SUDDEN
TERROR

SUDDEN TERROR

Exposing *Militant* Islam's War
Against the United States and Israel

DR. DAVID FRIEDMAN

Lederer Books
a division of
Messianic Jewish Publishers

Unless otherwise indicated, Scripture quotations are taken from the *Complete Jewish Bible*, Copyright © 1998 by David H. Stern, published by Jewish New Testament Publications, Inc.

The following Bible version was also used:
The Holy Bible, New International Version, Copyright © 1984 by International Bible Society. Use by permission of Zondervan Publishing House.

Printed in the United States of America
Cover and interior design by Drawing Board Studios

06 05 04 03 02   9 8 7 6 5 4 3 2 1
ISBN 1-880226-15-4

Library of Congress Control Number: 2002108079

Lederer Books
a division of
Messianic Jewish Publishers
6204 Park Heights Ave.
Baltimore, Maryland 21215
(410) 358-6471

Distributed by
Messianic Jewish Resources International
Individual order line: (800) 410-7367
Trade order line: (800) 773-MJRI (6574)
E-mail: lederer@messianicjewish.net
Website: www.messianicjewish.net

DEDICATIONS

To Yitzhak Rabin: May his memory be blessed.

To Menachem Begin, Yitzhak Shamir, Binyamin Netanyahu, Ehud Barak, and Ariel Sharon, former and current Israeli Heads of State: They dedicated great efforts to battle terrorism.

To Todd Beamer: A victim of terrorism on United flight 93, which crashed in Pennsylvania. He fought back.

To Leon Klinghoffer: Too often a forgotten American victim of PLO terror. May his memory be blessed.

To Alice Kostrowa: A Polish WWII underground army nurse who befriended and cared for aging Polish Jewish Holocaust victims. She fought Nazi terror and has stood by the side of the Jewish people for more than sixty years.

To Nissim ben Shalom: A civil rights attorney who devoted his efforts to upholding the dignity of all human life. He instilled a love of justice in me. May his memory be blessed.

To Yehudah Traub: My colleague, murdered in a terrorist attack while bringing food to his friends. May his memory be blessed.

To the victims and families of the 1998 American Embassy bombings in Kenya and Tanzania: May you be comforted.

Lastly, to Grzegorz Tisch: He saved the lives of my people in Nazi-occupied Poland, and, at age ninety-two, whispered to me with tearful eyes, "I would do it again."

All of you define the word *hero*.

CONTENTS

INTRODUCTION

The lethal attacks of September 11, 2001 forced the United States to enter the world of terrorism, as victims, on a scale previously unknown. Americans can gain a great deal of comfort and guidance as they come to understand Israel's lengthy history in this fight. The United States and Israel have been political allies for fifty-four years. In times like these, we can help one another.

As an Israeli who sympathizes with America's ideals of freedom and democracy, I feel great sorrow and pain over the attacks the United States endured. On September 11, 2001, Israel declared a national day of mourning, in solidarity with the American people. Flags flew at half-mast and radio stations played somber music. Israelis grieved over the murder of innocent Americans. Israeli Prime Minister Ariel Sharon responded:

> On behalf of the people of Israel, I wish to send our deepest condolences and heartfelt sympathy to the American people, President Bush and the entire U.S. government, following the terror attacks against the U.S. and our common values.... At this most difficult hour, all Israelis stand as one with the American people. Our hearts are with you, and we are ready to provide any assistance at any time.[1]

Israel's equivalent of the Red Cross, the *Magen David Adom* (Hebrew, Red Star of David) called on the public to donate blood. The Israeli people have endured four major conflicts, a war of attrition, constant ongoing terrorism, and numerous other military confrontations since 1948, all coming after the six-million-victim European Holocaust. Although Israel has not had four thousand citizens murdered during any one single attack, the over one thousand Israelis murdered or wounded by the Palestinian Authority (PA) since October 2000 is the numerical equivalent of 44,000 American casualties. This contrast should give a sense of the never-ending Israeli trauma.[2]

Israel's sympathy will continue. Former Prime Minister Binyamin Netanyahu commented to the press, "I speak for all Israelis in saying that the hearts of Israelis are broken by this tragedy."[3]

As America's war on terror intensifies, the same struggle persists in Israel. Since the September 11 attacks on New York and Washington D.C., Israel has continued to suffer non-stop terrorist attacks. The struggle that America is just now experiencing has been plaguing Israel for many years. This war against terrorism links our peoples together in new ways. We share a common enemy whose goal is the destruction of our societies.

The majority of Muslims worldwide are not extremists. They do not share the views of those who carried out the acts that felled the World Trade Center and destroyed a section of the Pentagon. Yet, in the Middle East, a financially affluent, radical, militant Muslim movement rapidly gains converts. This movement has been termed *fundamentalist Islam* and is represented by organizations that sponsor international terrorism.

Unfortunately, Arab states such as Syria, Libya, and Iraq harbor and fund such movements. Taliban-ruled Afghanistan supported Osama bin Laden and his *Al-Qa'eda* organization. Iran, though not an Arab state, sponsors, finances, and recruits on behalf of the *Hizballah* organization. A number of former Soviet states in Central Asia are suspected of abetting international terrorism. If the democratic world is to be made safer, this network of terrorism must be fought and defeated. Israel has known this for quite some time.

This book seeks to educate the average American citizen about a very real threat. I have not provided a comprehensive account of all aspects of either the American or Israeli struggle. My reflections are designed to present the sober reality of America's situation vis-à-vis Arab and Muslim-sponsored terrorism. As someone who has lived through that reality, my goal is to awaken readers to what may lie ahead and offer hope that a common enemy can be defeated.

I respect the Arab culture and Arab society. My problem is not with the Arab peoples per se. Neither is it with Islam. I believe in freedom of religious belief. My problem, as I argue in this work, is with the dictatorial regimes that rule over most Arab nations today. These governments allow a hatred of America and Israel to foment in their nations. Additionally, the growth of a militant, anti-Jewish, anti-Christian, fundamentalist Islam is a force that threatens Western civilization. Some Muslim spokesmen, such as Professor Khan in the United States and Sheikh Palazzi in Italy, have disassociated themselves with the type of violence and hatred advocated by the Osama bin Ladens and Yassir Arafats of this world. I applaud their stands. I do not desire to encourage the hatred of Arab people or Muslims as a religious group. Any who read this book in that light read my intent wrongly. My goal is to expose the politics, beliefs, and machinations of those who advocate the violent destruction of the United States and Israel, and to encourage Americans to work with Israel in the war against terrorism.

Chapter One

MY EXPERIENCES WITH TERRORISM

Past Encounters

According to the Jewish calendar, each new day begins at sundown. Yom Kippur (the Day of Atonement) is one of the holiest days of the Jewish year. In 1995, on the afternoon before this important day began, I was in Jerusalem and away from home. I wanted to get back to my family for Yom Kippur so we could attend evening prayers at the synagogue. While driving home, about an hour away from my destination and hurrying to beat the sacred day's arrival, I saw an abandoned car in front of me. It was turned sideways, blocking the road. An Israeli soldier stood nearby, stopping all traffic. He told me that the bomb squad was on its way to search for hidden explosives. Dozens of cars were lined up, unable to move until the crew could check the vehicle in question and pronounce it safe for us to pass by. This process could have taken hours. I did not want to wait that long.

I asked the soldier if he knew an alternate route beyond the roadblock. He gave me directions and pointed out a detour in the distance. Along with a line of cars also trying to get by, I drove the small, rocky path, meandering through an olive orchard outside an Arab village. From the license plates of the other cars on the road, I could tell that I was the only Jewish traveler. (Vehicles owned by Israelis are yellow, while Arab licenses are white or blue.) It was a tense time. Recently, there had been a number of anti-Israeli incidents in the area. Arab terrorists had surrounded Jewish vehicles, rocking them back and forth to turn them over, and lighting them on fire. The ensuing explosions maimed and killed the occupants of these cars.

I wanted to get back among other Israeli cars as quickly as possible but I was only able to move about five miles an hour. I was feeling relieved as I approached the end of the detour, near the hook-up to the main road. Suddenly, a black Mercedes Benz approached from the opposite direction. It turned sideways to block my car. Six young Arab men in leather jackets jumped out and rushed at me. One put his face very close to my windshield and shouted, "We don't let Jews pass by on this road." Gripped with fear, I waited a second, hoping they would back down, but instead, they surrounded my car, despite the silent Arab witnesses sitting in their vehicles behind us. These men were not afraid of onlookers from among their own people. Because of my work, I carried a weapon at all times and took the only action possible.

Bursting out of my car, I pulled my gun and pointed it at my attackers. Abruptly, all six men jumped back into the Mercedes. They straightened their car, kicked it into reverse, and flew onto the main road in the opposite direction. God had mercy on me. I made it home to my family, more thankful than ever to see the faces of my wife and children. I heard *Kol Nidre* (opening prayer of the Yom Kippur service) sung that evening.

I often wonder what would have become of me if I did not have that gun. I don't know why the six men didn't pursue me. Maybe they weren't armed, or were under orders not to use firearms or start a shooting incident. I'll never know.

The first *intifada* (Arabic, uprising) began in December 1987 and lasted until September 1993). In my neighborhood, stones were hurled daily at passing Jewish cars. One rainy day, I left home early to attend a conference in Tel Aviv, an hour from my town. Despite the bad weather, visibility was good and traffic was moving freely. After driving for about fifteen minutes, I rounded a bend. I noticed an oily black substance on the pavement but before I had time to react, my car went out of control and I careened off the road, skidding wildly to the right over a small shoulder. The car flipped and stopped only after becoming wedged against the side of a rocky hill. I was not seriously injured, but my car was crushed and had to be towed away. "This isn't rare, don't worry about it, you're alive," the tow truck driver remarked. "Everyone in town has their spot on *this* road."

Apparently, I hit an oil spill. Sometimes, the first rains of the year are dangerous; the rainwater mixes with oil on the road and causes a slippery residue. However, it had already rained that year. Although I came out of that experience bruised, shaken up, and without a car, I was alive, and grateful to God. Had my vehicle slid into the oncoming traffic, this story would have had a tragic ending.

My supervisor at work informed me that on the morning of this accident, Arab terrorists had spilled oil from the back of a truck at strategic spots in order to cause such mishaps. Another car had gone out of control at the same spot, sliding into oncoming traffic. The driver had been killed.

That same year, my wife went to her physician for a checkup. As she was driving home a few hours later, something hit the car, causing it to thrust forward. After smashing against the vehicle, the object bounced off and exploded. She checked the rear view mirror and saw a smoking, flaming bottle in the road behind her. Someone had hurled a Molotov cocktail from the ditch beside the road. After rushing home, she frantically told me what happened.

Not long afterward, my wife was driving between two ridges on the very same road, going in the opposite direction. All of a sudden, a hail of rocks hit the windshield, damaging it. Though my wife was physically unharmed, this event caused some emotional trauma. Rocks hurled at oncoming cars can easily kill drivers and passengers, depending upon the speed of the vehicle. Rock throwing is not a harmless children's game.

One evening, in the winter of 1994, I was driving on a dark road on my way home from work. Suddenly, about a half-hour away from my town, I saw movement in front of me but was unable to discern its source. Before I could figure it out, some kind of rolling object flew into the road in front of me. It seemed to be made out of wood and nails and I drove over it. One of my tires blew out. Afraid that more danger might await me if I stopped, I continued on, knowing that I might destroy my tire rim. I made it to a small Jewish village two kilometers down the road. The guard on duty helped me change my tire. He said a number of similar incidents had recently occurred on this same road, ostensibly, to harm Israeli commuters. Sometimes at night, he added, he could hear people laughing in the distance after an attack on an Israeli motorist had occurred.

In 1996, two Jerusalem city buses filled with students were on their way to the Hebrew University. My cousin, a woman in her midthirties and slightly paralyzed, was among the passengers. She had just started graduate school. Without forewarning, there was a powerful explosion. The next thing my cousin knew, she was in a bed at Sha'are Tzedek Hospital. One of her shoulders had been torn off. Physicians were unsure if they would be able to save her arm. Hundreds of tiny shards of glass were embedded in her skin. According to her doctors, these shards could not be removed. Arab suicide bombers had blown up the busses. When I visited my cousin in the hospital, she did not recognize me nor could she recall getting on that bus. Two weeks had already passed, though she remembered nothing about the incident.

Her elderly mother, a survivor of four wars, was a political "dove" and despised all forms of violence. She had heartily backed the Oslo Accords and the immediate recognition of a Palestinian state. She believed in the dignity of all people. Throughout her life, she supported Israeli political appeasement wherever and whenever possible. But now, she sat on the edge of her daughter's bed with tears in her eyes. Her politics had not helped to avert this tragedy. The assassins had made no concessions for peace seekers. *In fact, these Arab terrorists had also murdered some of their own people.* In crowds or on buses, these cold-blooded murderers cannot restrict their killing to specific victims.

In September 1997, while in the army reserves, I had a one-day assignment in Tel Aviv. My regular office was in downtown Jerusalem. While away at the military briefing, one of our officers received a report of a *pig'ua* (Hebrew, violent incident). When he informed us of the place of the incident, I realized that it was the very street corner on which my office was located. We quickly disbanded and immediately headed for Jerusalem to offer help to the victims. Muslim suicide bombers had blown themselves up on one of Jerusalem's busiest streets at three o'clock in the afternoon. Eight people were murdered. The street was covered with shattered glass and broken furniture.

One of our office employees was missing. She had been sent on an errand about the time of the explosion. The office administrator had to go through eight body bags to search for her. He saw torn body parts and mangled corpses. Blood and human flesh stuck to adjacent building walls. It was a gruesome sight. Our absent co-worker, a secretary, was not among the victims. We were thankful when she telephoned to let us know that she was safe in another area of the city. The police had prevented her from returning to the office to ensure her safety. Our office administrator later described the attack:

It was a beautiful September afternoon in Jerusalem. The sun was hot in the sky and the air was heavy with the heat. I was on my way down the steps to a meeting after talking with two friends about some small business issues when someone told me I had an incoming telephone call. That call may have saved my life. My office was situated on the third floor of a building off Ben Yehudah St. in the heart of Jerusalem. I'd just sat down to receive my call when I heard the first explosion. Two others followed quickly, the last being close enough that it shook the plaster off of the ceiling in my office. The noise from the blasts had hardly died down when the sound of alarms filled the air. Each of us knew what had happened. I immediately started down the stairs to see how I might be able to help. As I emerged onto the street, the scene that stretched before me overcame me. The air was filled with smoke and dust, people were running in every direction, screams filled the air, and most horrific, bodies were strewn like discarded dolls. People sat dazed and bleeding. Almost immediately, an Israeli soldier met me and firmly ordered me back inside my office building, saying there was still a danger of yet further blasts. I returned upstairs and gathered with other office members on the veranda to watch the scene below us. What looked to be the body of a woman was lying in front of the bank across the street from us. There were no arms and only one leg, but from the long hair, we were sure it was an older lady who had died. Only later did we learn that it was the body of one of the suicide bombers. He and his accomplices had disguised themselves as elderly people so as not to draw any attention to themselves as they carried out their cowardly act. We watched as the army began to collect the bodies of the dead, mostly children who had come to downtown Jerusalem to buy their school supplies for the coming academic year. We watched as the local hevrat kadishah [Hebrew, burial society workers] arrived to go about the horrible task of collecting each body part, or even blood that had been spilled, for a proper burial. All the while the question kept racing through my mind—why? The innocent victims were just children, Jewish children, on their way to buy supplies for school.[1]

Although still in shock, that night, I took the office administrator to a café. We wanted to talk about the horrific events in an attempt to assuage some of our grief. We spent most of that evening in silence as we stared at our coffee cups. Only one thought was foremost in our minds. Whoever had carried out this attack was not worthy of being called a human.

Every Israeli community in which I have lived has been touched by the horror of terrorism. In a peaceful Tel Aviv suburb where I once resided, an armed Arab agricultural laborer stabbed a young Israeli teen as he was walking home from school. Though wounded, the teen escaped. When I lived north of Jerusalem, my neighbor, a United States Marine veteran and immigrant to Israel, was knifed to death by Arab youths while taking a Sabbath walk. His murderers had just eaten a meal with him. In a nearby locale, months later, an Israeli was murdered in his bed at dawn. The assassin, from a surrounding Arab village, broke into the man's house and stole nothing—he just committed the murder and fled.

Two other incidents, occurring ten years apart, directly affected me. While studying at the Hebrew University in Jerusalem in the late 1970s, I took a break and walked to a small park on the Mount of Olives. I was seeking a moment of peace and quiet. Two Arab boys, not more than six or seven years old, began throwing rocks at me. I looked into their eyes and saw a burning hatred, a ferocity of spirit that little children should never experience. I can only guess what they had been taught about Israelis and Jews.

Another time, in the late 1980s, my wife and children were in the Galilee, at a park just off the main road. My wife parked the car and two of our sons, both not yet six years old, went to find a place to have a picnic. An Arab family with a young child was nearby. Suddenly, the child picked up some rocks, went over to my wife, and threw them at her and at my parked car. My family was physically unharmed, though stunned by such loathing from such a young child. Someone was teaching this child to hate Jews. Hatred breeds terrorism. *Only God's mercy can stop the rocks from becoming bullets and bombs in the years ahead.*

The Present Situation

I now live in Jerusalem. The number of incidents which occur here every year are too many to recount. Students and colleagues of mine have been killed. Children of friends have been murdered. The terrorists' objective is intimidation. They seek to murder as well as frighten innocent people. They desire to cause panic, chaos, and a sense of societal instability. This will discourage Israelis and cause some to contemplate emigration. In America, the terrorists' goals are much the same.

Israeli citizens are engaged in a daily war on terror. Therefore, it was natural for me, and all Israelis, to feel deep sympathy for the United States on September 11. We have lived with the threat of terrorism since *before* our state's inception in 1948. For this very reason, we have continually pleaded with worldwide governments to recognize the necessity of our proactive response. Too often, people who have never lived with the reality of terrorism criticize Israeli counter-measures. Murdered children, shattered lives, and families forever torn apart . . . this kind of suffering is too familiar to Israelis. From the beginning of the second *intifada* in September 2000 to the end of May 2002, 502 Israelis were killed by Palestinian attacks. Close to 4027 citizens were injured.[2] These numbers rise daily.

Americans, now tasting radical Muslim terror as never before, have the prayers and sympathy of Israelis. I was heartened when Israel volunteered dog-led rescue squads to help search for September 11 survivors. (Ultimately, they were not used.) Israel aided America with rescue squads when the embassy in Kenya was struck in 1998. President Arap Moi of Kenya and former President Clinton acknowledged Israel's humanitarian contribution in that operation, which led to the rescue of three survivors. Israel was ready to assist America in the struggle then, and she will *always* be ready to help.

In contrast, the Palestinian population's reaction to events on September 11 was sad and revealing. Despite Mr. Arafat's denunciation of the attack, spontaneous celebrations broke out in Judea, Samaria, Gaza, and Lebanon. These displays of rejoicing demonstrated a harsh truth—the fact that many Palestinians consider the United States a deserving target, even though the country had been a main financier of the Palestinian Authority infrastructure. Why didn't Mr. Arafat, or any Palestinian Authority public figure, condemn these celebrations? *Why didn't Mr. Arafat call on his people to stop mocking the American tragedy?* Clearly, he is more concerned with damage control than with morality. Several Palestinian Christians voiced sympathy for the United States after the attacks. However, their voices were not heard among their own people, and their sentiments did not represent the majority viewpoint.

Israeli taxes, weapons, food, and medicines have been used to help support and finance the PA infrastructure since the signing of the Oslo Accords in September 1993. The Oslo Accords are an agreement between Israel and the PA to normalize relations and work towards a full peace. The Palestinian uprising against Israel reflects a total lack of appreciation of Israeli assistance. My tax payments went to help finance their government and pay for weapons that were given to their police force—a force that resembles an army. (In Gaza, they held twice the amount of weapons legally allowed in the Oslo Accords.) Many of these weapons, donated by Israel, *have been used against Israeli citizens*. After the second *intifada* began, Israel *still* continued to contribute food and medicine to help the Palestinians.

The Palestinians show the same disdain for American contributions. The United States, a country that helped to resurrect Yassir Arafat's faltering political career, and was the main financier of the Palestinian infrastructure, found herself being mocked in Palestinian celebrations after the vicious attacks against her innocent citizens.

President George W. Bush recognizes Israel as an ally and a partner in the war against terrorism. Only through cooperation can our two nations achieve the results that can help stave off future terrorist attacks. Israel can assist the United States, and the United States can and should stand by Israel. Israeli success is vital to America's struggle. May God help us win this war. The issue at stake, as expressed so well by President Bush, is the survival of civilization; not just Western civilization, but of all mankind.[3]

On March 8, 2002, Israel ended its military thrust in the Deheisha refugee camp. Its objective and method of operation were similar to America's Operation Anaconda, carried out in Afghanistan during the same period. Over six hundred Palestinians from the *Al-Aksa* Brigade of the *Fatah*, and from *Hamas*, *Tanzim*, and the Islamic *Jihad* group, were disarmed, their caches of weapons captured. A *Hamas* artillery laboratory containing ten rockets, ready to be used in anti-Israeli activity, was shut down. After this raid, a similar assault was made on the Jabaliyya refugee camp in the Gaza Strip. Based upon my own experiences in that same Gaza camp fifteen years ago, I know that many of the inhabitants have been involved in terrorist activities for a long time.

Fundamentalist Muslim spokespersons such as Abdel Aziz Rantisi, one of the leaders of *Hamas*, will claim that the current *intifada* is the only way to stop Israel from its campaign in Jabaliyya. However, the same murderous attitude existed in the first *intifada*. It also existed before Israel became a state. In 1929, Arab rioters, in what was then known as "Mandated Palestine," sought to annihilate Jews. Continual Arab assaults against *kibbutzim* (communal farming societies) necessitated that the Jewish communities organize themselves for self-defense. A military defense unit, named the *Haganah* (Hebrew, defense), was thus formed. It was incorporated into the Israel Defense Forces.

Our current crisis is the consequence of a long history of conflict. It is not the result of Israel's incursion into refugee camps or anywhere else.

Chapter Two

THE TORAH ON THE ARAB PEOPLES

The perpetrators of the dastardly deeds of September 11, 2001 were ethnic Arabs. Most were Saudi citizens and believers in a violent fundamentalist form of Islam. Therefore, it is worthwhile, for Jews and Christians alike, to examine the Torah (Hebrew, Bible) to learn about the beginnings of the Arab people.

Many Israelis descend from biblical figures. DNA testing to determine the possibility of a priestly background reveals a common gene pool among those thought to be descendants of this line. Additionally, the preservation of ancient Hebrew family names may reveal biblical tribal affiliations. For example, the surnames Cohen, Levi, Levine, Kahn, and Kaplan all indicate a priestly or Levitical lineage.

In the Arab world, a similar situation may exist. Some ethnic Arabs descend from the Torah's progenitors. However, the genealogies of both peoples include those who are not direct descendants of those biblical figures considered the "fathers" of our two peoples. For example, many converts to Judaism in Russia belonged to the Khazar Kingdom. Their descendants may still practice Judaism. In the ancient Mediterranean world, many converts to Judaism came from Roman Empire. All of these converts (and their progeny) would not have been blood descendants of Avraham (Abraham), Yitz'chak (Isaac) and Ya'akov (Jacob).

Similarly, the Arab peoples are not a homogenous ethnic group. Much intermarriage has taken place in the Arab world, especially since the advent of Islam. Furthermore, the Muslim world is not comprised of one distinct people group. Many Arabs, Indians, Pakistanis, Iranians, Malaysians, Indonesians, as well as other nationalities can be counted among them. Examining the Torah can provide an understanding of the progenitors of the Jewish and Arab peoples, although it is nearly impossible to establish claims of pure descent from the biblical "fathers." Through God's oversight, the Jewish people continue to exist, as promised in the covenant with Avraham.

The Arabs also live on today, even if no clear proof of descent from Yishma'el (Hebrew, Ishmael) can be found.

A passage from the Book of Genesis reveals the beginning of the Arab people:

> Now God said to Avram, "Get yourself out of your country, away from your kinsmen and away from your father's house, and to the land that I will show you. I will bless you and make your name great; and you are to be a blessing." (Gen. 12:1–2, author's translation)

God separated Avram from every other person on the face of the earth by giving him unconditional promises linked to a blood covenant. When he reached old age, Avram was distressed because he did not have a son to inherit God's covenant promises, so he fathered a son through his wife's servant-girl.

> Hagar bore Avram a son, and Avram called the son whom Hagar had borne Yishma'el. (Gen. 16:15)

According to the Torah, God did *not* mean to bestow his covenant promises on this son after Avram's death. (At this point in the Torah, God changes Avram's name to Avraham.) Through the fulfillment of another one of God's promises, Sarah and Avraham rejoice in unlikely birth of a son in their old age, whom they name *Yitz'chak*. It is this son, Yitz'chak, who becomes the heir to the covenant promises God made to Avraham.

Genesis 21:9–10 sheds light on what happens later:

> But Sarah saw the son of Hagar the Egyptian, whom Hagar had borne to Avraham, making fun of [Sarah's son] Yitz'chak, so Sarah said to Avraham, "Throw this slave-girl out! And her son! I will not have this slave-girl's son as your heir along with my son Yitz'chak."

Avraham took similar actions with his other sons:

> Avraham gave everything he owned to Yitz'chak. But to the sons of the concubines, he made grants while he was still living and sent them off to the east, to the land of Kedem, away from Yitz'chak his son. (Gen. 25:5–6)

In spite of the fact that Yishma'el was forcefully separated from his father's house, he did have later contact with Yitz'chak, as the Torah records them as being present at the burial of their father (Gen. 25:9).

Yishma'el is generally considered to be the progenitor of the Arab peoples. Yitz'chak is seen in the Torah as Avraham's son and inheritor of the promises of the special covenant between Avraham and God. This situation *excluded* having any other inheritors from among his brothers (i.e., other sons born to Avraham). *No other son of Avraham could receive the special covenant promises that God gave to Avraham.* The Torah affirms this truth in these words:

> God said to Avraham, "Don't be distressed because of the boy and your slave girl. Listen to everything Sarah says to you [to expel Yishma'el and his mother from Yitz'chak's presence], because your descendants through Yitz'chak will be counted as the inheritors of my covenant promises. But I will also make a nation from the son of the slave-girl, since he is descended from you." (Gen. 21:12–13, author's translation)

Yitz'chak is the son through whom the "counting" mentioned in verses 12 and 13 will be done. The Hebrew phrase used to describe this, *ki b'yitzhak yikare leka zara* can literally be rendered, "Because your progeny will be called through Yitz'chak" (author's translation). That is, the covenant promises of God will be called [into being, as it were; passed on to the next generation] by way of Yitz'chak.

> I am establishing my covenant between me and you, along with your descendants after you, generation after generation, as an everlasting covenant. . . . Sarah your wife will bear you a son, and you are to call him Yitz'chak [laughter]. I will establish my covenant with him as an everlasting covenant for his descendants after him. But as for Yishma'el, I have heard you. I have blessed him. I will make him fruitful and give him many descendants. . . . But I will establish my covenant with Yitz'chak (Gen. 17:7a, 19b–21a)

Thus, Yitz'chak is given the role of inheritor of the covenant that God gave to his father Avraham. Yishma'el, too, as a son of Avraham, had special promises that were applicable only to him. However, the promises of God to each of these sons were *distinct and separate.*

Since Yitz'chak is the one who is given the "everlasting covenant" mentioned in chapter 17, it follows that Yitz'chak's descendants are the inheritors of the covenant between Avraham and God. God honored both Yitz'chak and Yishma'el, giving them each a special status. One inherited the everlasting covenant; the other was to be fruitful and numerous, bearing descendants who would form and rule kingdoms. Additionally, we see that is the descendants of Avraham who will be slaves in Egypt and inherit the promised everlasting covenant.

> Know this for certain: your descendants will be foreigners in a land that is not theirs. They will be slaves and held in oppression there four hundred years. (Gen. 15:13)

Today, the Jewish people consider themselves the descendants of those who experienced Egyptian slavery. The memory of this servitude is alive in our rituals, holidays, and prayers, and has been part of our culture for some 3,300 years. The experience is implanted in our collective historic consciousness. No other people group claims to be physically descended from the Hebrew slaves.

The Torah also makes it clear that Yitz'chak and *his descendants* inherited Avraham's covenant with God. The Almighty spoke with Moshe (Moses), shortly before the leader's death:

> ADONAI said to him, "This is the land concerning which I swore to Avraham, Yitz'chak and Ya'akov, 'I will give it to your descendants.' I have let you see it with your eyes, but you will not cross over there." (Deut. 34:4a)

The conveyance of the covenant promises goes through Avraham, Yitz'chak, and Ya'akov. I am not belaboring the distinctions between the two sons to prove that Yitz'chak is humanly superior to Yishma'el. However, the differences between the two sons need to be understood. The Bible records other circumstances where this type of delineation occurred along genealogical lines. In fact, Yitz'chak's sons, Ya'akov and Esav (Esau), were part of such a situation. Ya'akov received the highest blessing of his father, Yitz'chak:

> "May peoples serve you and nations bow down to you. May you be lord over your kinsmen, let your mother's descen-

dants bow down to you. Cursed be everyone who curses you, and blessed be everyone who blesses you!" (Gen. 27:29)

Yitz'chak's other son, Esav, received a lesser blessing:

"Your home will be of the richness of the earth and of the dew of heaven from above. You will live by your sword, and you will serve your brother. But when you break loose, you will shake his yoke off your neck. (Gen. 27:39b–40)

Thus, one son, Ya'akov, would have descendants who would be pre-eminent, while the other son, Esav, would have progeny who would take a lesser role. Even today, Ya'akov's descendants continue to live and prosper, while Esav's descendants (the ancient Edomite nation) died out millennia ago. Avraham's covenant promises with God are passed on from Yitz'chak to Ya'akov, as opposed to Esav. Gen. 28:3–4 emphasizes this point:

"May El Shaddai [Almighty God] bless you [Ya'akov], make you fruitful and increase your descendants . . . may he give you the blessing which he gave Avraham, you and your descendants with you, so that you will possess the land you will travel through, the land God gave to Avraham."

Such genealogical demarcations served to separate people so they could fulfill their God-given functions. Here, Ya'akov received the covenant promises of his father and grandfather, while Esav was disqualified from receiving these blessings. This situation is different from the case of Yitz'chak and Yishma'el, i.e., Esav is considered evil, while Yishma'el is not portrayed as a wicked person.

Although Yishma'el, the traditional father of the Arab peoples, is given an honored role in the Torah, he was not privy to the everlasting covenant that his half-brother inherited. Indeed, as God had promised, Yishma'el's fruitfulness is clear:

Here is the genealogy of Yishma'el, Avraham's son . . . these are the names of the sons of Yishma'el . . . Nevayot . . . Kedar, Adbe'el, Mivsam, Mishma, Duman, Massa, Hadad, Teima, Yetur, Nafish and Kedmah . . . and Yishma'el's sons lived between Havilah and Shur, near Egypt, as you go toward Ashur. (Gen. 25:12–15, 18a, author's translation)

However, the Torah also portrays Yishma'el in a negative light. He is described as a warlike, contentious person.

> And he will be a wild man: he will struggle against everyone, and everyone will struggle with him. He will live close to his brothers. (Gen. 16:12, author's translation)

But would Yishma'el's descendants would automatically inherit these behavioral traits? The only evidence to support this premise is found in Genesis 25:18:

> His [Yishma'el's] descendants settled in the area from Havilah to Shur, near the border of Egypt, as you go toward Asshur. And they lived in hostility toward all their brothers. (NIV)

The phrase "his brothers" may refer to Yishma'el's half-brothers, the sons born to Avraham by his wife Keturah (and possibly other concubines). Genesis 25:1–3 provides a list of six such half-brothers. Although we learn that his clan acted in a hostile manner, the Torah *does not* tell us that all of Yishma'el's descendants will automatically inherit this behavioral trait. Such a conclusion would be prejudicial and would be taking the verse out of context. According to the text, Yishma'el's descendants increased and settled in specific region.

There is no condemnation of Yishma'el and his descendants in the Book of Genesis. The God of Israel promised that blessings and fruitfulness would come to his genealogical line. Yishma'el's descendants do not disappear from the biblical account, but they are never a focal point. Rather, the acts of the God of Israel in the lives of the major figures of the *genealogical line of Avraham through Yitz'chak* becomes the center of attention in the ensuing narrative.

Traditional Judaism does not look upon those who claim to be Yishma'el's descendants with any theological disdain. However, the relationship between the Jewish and Arab peoples has been volatile, particularly after the advent of Islam. Yet, no precept of the Torah provides justification for despising the Arab people. This is in contrast to interpretations of the *Qur'an* made by factions of the Muslim fundamentalist movement. Such interpretations teach that Jews and Christians are the absolute enemies of Allah. A more moderate reading of the *Qur'an* leads to less hateful conclusions.

For many years, there was an atmosphere of acceptance between my people and our Muslim neighbors. Half a dozen Arab villages surrounded my town. In the early 1980s, it was possible to shop in these villages and eat in their restaurants. Israelis were often invited to Arab homes. My town employed some three hundred Arab workers. The differences between our cultures and religions did not prevent us from treating each other with honor and dignity. This demonstrated the fact that it *is* possible for Israelis and Muslims to live in peace. There does not have to be an interpretation of the *Qur'an* that denigrates the value of Jewish lives. Most Israelis uphold the worth of all lives, including those of our Arabs and Muslim neighbors.

Although the nation of Israel has been forced into a defensive mode in order to survive, the words of the prophet Isaiah provide hope for the future:

> On that day Israel will be a third partner with Egypt and Ashur, a blessing here on earth; for ADONAI-*Tzva'ot* [LORD of Hosts] has blessed him: "Blessed be Egypt my people, Ashur, the work of my hands and Isra'el my heritage." (Isa. 19:24–25)

In spite of the continuing war against terrorism, one day, Isaiah's words will be a reality, and peace will prevail in the region. May the Holy One of Israel bring that era soon!

Chapter Three

A NEW RELIGION TAKES ROOT

To properly analyze the roots of militant Islamic terror, it is crucial to examine the religious aspects of the issue. It is a difficult subject to approach because the results of such an examination may run counter to what is considered politically correct in the Western world. I do not denigrate the religion of Islam. Muslims have a right to believe in and practice their faith, both in Israel and in the United States. The Israeli Declaration of Independence upholds the right of Muslims to worship freely, and Israelis have never sought to suppress those rights. Yet, many Muslims in today's Middle East are becoming increasingly intolerant of the rights of others.

Radical Muslims often interpret verses recited by Muhammad against ancient Medina's Jewish clans as applicable to modern Jews. These types of Qur'anic applications can lead to a virulent hatred of the state of Israel. Examining some of these verses will shed light on their use as fuel for this escalating animosity.

The Beginning of Islam

Muhammad, the founder of Islam, was born in 570 c.e., in Mecca, which is in present day Saudi Arabia. Orphaned at an early age, he was first raised by his grandfather, and then his uncle, Abu Talib. In 595, he married a forty-year old woman named Khadija. Mecca had been a pilgrimage center for pagan religious practices. Such pilgrimages focused on the black Kaba rock, which is still a shrine today. In the year 610, possibly on the 26th day of the month of Ramadan, Muhammad experienced what is known as the "night of power." While at a cave by Mt. Hira, he had a series of visions and heard voices, which he took to be from the one single deity (Allah). In some sense, the story resembles that of Moshe in the Torah, who heard instructions from the God of Israel in the Sinai wilderness.

Muhammad's belief that Allah had called him to become a prophet is also reminiscent of Moshe's call by God:

> [Muhammad stated] "The angel caught me (forcefully) and pressed me so hard that I could not bear it any more. He then released me and again asked me to [recite and read his revelations publicly] and I replied, 'I do not know how to read.' Thereupon he caught me again and pressed me a second time till I could not bear it anymore. He then released me and again asked me to read but again I replied, 'I do not know how to read (or what shall I read)?' Thereupon he caught me for the third time and pressed me, and then released me and said, 'Read in the name of your Lord, who has created all that exists, has created man from a clot. Read! And your Lord is the Most Generous.'" (Sahih Bukhari, Volume 1, Book 1, Number 3)[1]

Some 1800 years before Muhammad, the God of Israel called Moshe to lead the Jewish people, and to help free them from slavery in Egypt. The similarity between the encounters of these two men is uncanny. The Bible states:

> And Moshe was the shepherd of the flocks of Yitro [Jethro] his father-in-law, the priest of Midian; and he led the flocks to a far end of the wilderness and arrived at Mt. Horeb, God's mountain. And the angel of God appeared to him in a flame of fire from the midst of a bush. Moshe looked and the bush burned in fire, but it did not burn up. So Moshe said, "I'll give attention to this and look further at this incredible phenomenon, and see why the bush is not burning up." And God saw that Moshe was concerned with seeing this, so he called to him from the bush, and said, "Moshe, Moshe, " and he answered, "Here I am." . . . And Moshe said to God, "Who am I, that I should . . . lead Israel out of Egypt?" . . . Moshe answered God, "O Lord, I am not a man of many words, not till now, nor since You have spoken to [me] . . . for I am a man of slow speech and of a slow tongue." And the Lord said to him, "Who makes a man dumb or deaf, or seeing or blind? Is it not I the Lord. Now go, and I will be with your mouth, and teach you what you will say." (Exod. 3:1–4, 11, 4:10–12, author's translation)

In both narratives, the deity appears to shepherds in a pastoral setting. He identifies himself and gives instructions about what to do next. Both men voice protests to the message of their deity, are rebuked for their objections, then further encouraged to obey the message given. Although the narratives are alike in theme, setting, and content, we cannot conclude that Muhammad purposely borrowed anything from the Torah.

We do know that Muhammad took aspects of Jewish life and adapted them for his own use. For example, he instructed his early followers to pray facing Jerusalem, as was the custom of the Jewish people. After his relations with Medina's Jewish tribes soured, he commanded his followers to pray facing Mecca. In Arabic, this Islamic practice is known as the *qibla*.

In 613, Muhammad made his first public proclamations, as a result of his revelations. His most influential followers at Mecca, who rejected polytheism and accepted him as a prophet, were his wife, Khadija; his cousin, Waraka; his adopted son, Zaid; his nephew, Ali; a future father-in-law, Abu Bakr; his uncle, Hamza; and Utman bin Affan, a devoted follower.

Most of Mecca rejected Muhammad's revelations. He spent the next ten years attempting to convince his hometown of his call by Allah, as well as the validity of the religious doctrines he taught. The fact that politics and religion were mixed in Mecca, made the reception of his message all the more difficult. In other words, if Muhammad was Allah's prophet, then he must also be Mecca's political ruler. Indeed, he was offering Mecca political unity under one chief, and tribal unity through the adoption of one religion.

In 619, Khadija died, and the persecution in Mecca against Muhammad increased. He left for the settlement of at-Ta'if, where he continued to preach his message. However, he was rejected there as well and returned to Mecca. Again, his teachings were not accepted. Mecca's dominant tribe, the Quraysh, attempted to assassinate him. Finally, on the 20th of June, 622, Muhammad and about one hundred of his followers left Mecca for greener pastures in the town of Yatrib. In Arabic, this migration to Yatrib is called the *hijrah*, and serves as the starting date of the Muslim calendar. Hence, when one buys an Arabic newspaper anywhere in the Muslim world, it is dated from the time of the *hijrah*.

Yatrib was renamed Medina (Arabic, the city of [the prophet]). There, Muhammad's new faith spread quickly for several reasons. Medina had two rival tribes, the Aus and Kazraj. Both wanted to find a third, independent tribe to rule the city in order to bring a balance of power. Muhammad and his followers fit the bill. Additionally, the three major Jewish tribes in Medina had already influenced the city regarding monotheism. Possibly, because of this Jewish religious influence, Muhammad's monotheistic doctrines were not rejected in Medina, as they had been in Mecca.

From 622 to 630, there was continual warring between the followers of Muhammad in Medina and the Quraysh tribe in Mecca. Two significant military conflicts, the battles of Badr and Uhud, took place, with each side winning gaining one victory. Ultimately, Muhammad prevailed, defeating the Quraysh tribe in 627 and subsequently occupying Mecca in 630. Thus, Mecca and Medina were united under Muhammad. All of the inhabitants of both cities adopted his monotheistic religion. In 632, Muhammad died, and his father-in-law, Abu Bakr, became the *caliph* (Arabic, deputy or successor). The four caliphs who immediately succeeded Muhammad had an explosive impact on the spread of Islam in the Middle East.

The Spread of Islam after Muhammad

From 632–634, Abu Bakr ruled as the Caliph. On the home front, he was known for his ability to engage dissident Muslims in battle, defeat them, and then force them to live under his authority. He was also able to conquer parts of Persia and the Byzantine Empire, spreading his new religious faith along with his political rule. Upon Abu Bakr's death in 634, Umar became the Caliph, ruling for ten years, and also warring against the Byzantines and Persians. His greatest victory was the defeat of the entire Persian army. Utman, one of Muhammad's son-in-laws, was the next Caliph. An Umayyad (a different clan than that of previous caliphs), he was murdered because of rivalries within the ruling clique. Ali, Muhammad's nephew, became the new caliph. Egyptian Muslims, who resented his authority over them, eventually took his life. The Umayyads then seized the caliphate and moved Islam's governmental center from Medina to Damascus (Syria). Ali's adherents remained disenfranchised and formed a new wing of Islam, *Shi'ism*. A major branch of Islam today, it has doctrinal differences with more mainstream Muslims. (The population of Iran is largely *Shi'ite*.) The Umayyad Muslims became the models for most Islamic belief. Their practice became known as *Sunni' Islam*, a term now synonymous with mainstream Muslim faith.

These four caliphs expanded Muslim rule westward to Egypt (660), eastward to Persia (660), and northwest across Israel, Lebanon, and Syria (659–669). By 669, Morocco, Tunisia, Algeria, and Libya had all come under Umayyad Muslim domination. The Muslim faith spread to the conquered lands, and by the late seventh century, it blanketed the Middle East and North Africa. In 710, Tarik ibn Ziyyad, the Muslim governor of Tangiers, invaded Iberia from North Africa with an army of ten thousand soldiers, conquering the isle of Gibraltar. After the Muslim conquest of Iberia in 718, Abd-Al-Rahman, the military commander at that time, sought to bring the battle into Europe's heartland. However, in October 732, his forces were defeated at the Battle of Tours (modern-day France) by the Frankish army. The outcome of this confrontation, one of the most decisive military battles in all history, served to limit Muslim domination of Europe to Iberia (the Muslim-ruled state of *Al-Andalus*).

This brief chronology of Muhammad and his successors should give the reader a basic understanding of spread of the Islamic faith and the political power of its early leaders. The Arabic word *Islam* means "submission." This definition refers to the faith's central concept (i.e., when one submits to Islam's five central practices, then and only then, will there be true peace). A metaphysical, subjective, inner peace for the adherent is *not* primarily meant. Rather, the concept refers to a practical, day-to-day, peace between members of society.

Muslims consider the *Qur'an* to be their sacred, authoritative text. It consists of one 114 written chapters of Muhammad's revelations. Additionally, the *Hadith*, a collection of statements, teachings, and stories about Muhammad, written by his early associates, are still devoutly studied. However, these writings are not considered to be as holy as the Qur'an. Islam's basic tenets are a recitation of the *shahada* (Arabic, declaration making one a Muslim), prayer, almsgiving, fasting, and the *hajj* (pilgrimage to Mecca). These universal Muslim practices do not involve warring against Jews.

Muhammad and the People of the Book

The *Qur'an* describes contact between Muhammad and the Jewish communities of his locale. The late Pakistani scholar and leader of the *Jamaat-i-Islam* (Pakistani Muslim political party), Abu-Ala' Maud04i, notes the background of Muhammad's formulations regarding Medina's Jewish tribes:

... they had strayed away ... during the centuries of degeneration and had adopted many un-Islamic creeds, rites and
customs of which there was no mention and for which there
was no sanction in the Torah. Not only this: they had tam-
pered with the Torah by inserting their own explanations and
interpretations into its text. They had distorted even that part
of the Word of God which had remained intact in their
Scriptures and taken out of it the real spirit of true religion
and were now clinging to a lifeless frame of rituals. Conse-
quently their beliefs, their morals and their conduct had
gone to the lowest depths of degeneration. The pity is that
they were not only satisfied with their condition but loved to
cling to it. Besides this, they had no intention or inclination
to accept any kind of reform. So they became bitter enemies
of those who came to teach them the Right Way and did their
worst to defeat every such effort ... and [they] made religion
the sole monopoly of the children of Israel. This was their
religious condition when the Holy Prophet [Muhammad]
went to Al-Madinah and invited the Jews to the true
religion.[2]

Abu-Ala' Maududi reveals the Qur'anic view of Medina's Jewish
tribes. His negative reading of the text reflects the influence of the
fundamentalist wing of Islam to which he belongs. Without adequate contextualization, fundamentalist Muslims gain a very un-
complimentary picture of Judaism, which they transfer to Jewish
people today. Assessing the historical accuracy of Qur'anic assertions regarding the condition of Medina's Jews is an important issue
for those of us outside the fold of Islam,
        The second chapter of the Qur'an's, *Surat al-baqarah* (Arabic,
Chapter of the Cow), includes Muhammad's statements about the
Banu Qaynuqa, a Jewish clan from Medina. Verse 75 notes:

Do you [Muslims] hope that they will believe in you, when
some of them [Jewish rabbis] have already heard the word of
God, and knowingly perverted it, although they understood
its meaning? (Dawood translation)

This verse portrays the Jewish religious leaders as insincere in
their handling of the Torah. Verse 76 continues with this theme:

When they [Jews] meet the faithful [Muslims], they declare, "We, too, are believers, but when alone, they say to each other, must you [Jews] declare to them [Muslims] what God has revealed to you [to these Jews, about the description and qualities of Muhammad] . . . Have you [Jews] no sense?" (Dawood translation)

Again, the Jewish community is accused of being dishonest, of hiding the fact that Torah foretold the coming of Muhammad as a prophet. The condemnation continues in verse 77:

Do they [Jews] not know that God has knowledge of all they conceal and all that they reveal? (Dawood translation)

Here, the Jewish community is warned that hiding these prophecies will not escape Divine attention. The implication is that there will be a price to pay for this theological dishonesty.

Verse 105 of *Surat al-baqarah* states:

The unbelievers among the People of the Book [Jews and Christians], and the pagans, resent that any blessings should have been sent down to you from your Lord. But God chooses whom He will for his mercy. . . . (Dawood translation)

This verse implies that those Jews and Christians who would not accept Muhammad's message and convert to Islam, could not expect to receive any blessings from Allah. It is unclear whether this verse refers to blessings in the present world as well as in the world to come, or just in the present world. Both Jews and Christians are negatively categorized.

This same chapter of the *Qur'an* provides such fundamentalists with a hint of even more punishment to be meted out on Jewish people:

Many among the People of the Book [Jews and Christians] wish, through envy, to lead you back to unbelief, now that you have embraced the faith [become adherents of Islam] and the truth [of Muhammad's prophethood] has been made plain to them. Forgive them and bear with them until God makes known his will. . . . (verse 109, Dawood translation)

According to this verse, a number of Jews and Christians were attempting to persuade Muslims to renounce their belief in the prophethood of Muhammad. Muhammad told the early Muslims to forgive these attempts to dissuade. However, the possibility remained that Allah would still severely judge these Jews and Christians. The original Arabic states:

> ... *hatta ya'uta alla bi'amurihi* ... [until Allah will give his future command].

Hence, the withholding of severe judgment is a temporary situation. This "reprieve" will only last until Allah reveals his will for the Jews and Christians, who do not follow Muhammad's religious teachings or accept his political power. Indeed, Muhammad did pronounce more judgements upon the Jewish tribes of Medina. The Banu Al-Nadir were exiled from the city, and the Banu Qaynuqa and Banu Qurayza experienced varying levels of punishment on account of their opposition to Muhammad. With the exception of the Khaybar region, Jewish people were not welcomed in the Hijaz peninsula (today's Saudi Arabia), where Medina was located. Thus, the judgement of verse 109 involved death for those who strongly opposed Muhammad (the Banu Qurayza), and exile for the other two clans (the Banu Al-Nadir and the Banu Qaynuqa), who did not accept Muhammad as a prophet but were less active in their opposition to his politics.

Verse 89 of the same *sura* (chapter of the Qur'an) accuses Medina's Jewish tribes of concealing the truth about Muhammad being a prophet:

> And now that a book [the Qur'an] confirming their own has come to them from God, they deny it, although they know it to be the truth and have long prayed for help against the unbelievers. God's curse be upon them the infidels! (Dawood translation)

What was meant by this "curse" of Allah (Arabic, *fala'nat Allah*)? The treatment of Medina's Jewish tribes reveals the answer to this question—punishment by exile and murder. Jews and Christians were viewed as seditious and theologically dishonest. This is consistent with what today's radical Muslim terrorists think about Israelis and, now, Americans.

Similar images are created by verse 146:

Those to whom We gave the Scriptures [Jews and Christians]
know Our apostle as they know their own sons. But some of
them deliberately conceal the truth [qualities of Muhammad
written in the Torah and the Gospels]. (Dawood translation)

Here, both Jews and Christians are said to have hidden the truth
about Muhammad's role. Again, both groups are portrayed as being
dishonest. Even if the "some of them" in this verse is only referring
to religious leaders, when Muhammad decapitated all of the men of
the Banu Qurayza tribe, his victims included all adults and boys
above the age of puberty, not merely the rabbis.

The only Jews and Christians who were to be considered allies
and acceptable as equals in early Muslim society were those who
converted to Islam. Verse 121 notes:

Those to whom We have given the Book [Jewish individuals
embracing Islam], and who read it as it ought to be read,
truly believe in it; those that deny it will surely be the losers.
(Dawood translation)

Since the vast majority of Jewish families in the Hijaz peninsula
refused to accept Muhammad's religious faith as well as his political
power, they could never be accepted as equal members of society.
They were the *al-chasiruna* (Arabic, losers). What did it mean to be a
part of this group? Again, the answer can be found by looking at what
happened to the three Jewish tribes of Medina. Examining subsequent
history can also help to define the meaning of this term. Those who
rejected Islam became *dhimmi* (Arabic, subjugated people), and responsible for paying the *jizya*, a tax for *dhimmi* communities. The
dhimmi lived without equal status in society and were subject to the
political whims of the ruling Muslim class. Because of their *dhimmi*
status throughout history, the Jewish people suffered much persecution at the hands of Muslim governments.

In *Surat al-Jumua*, (Arabic, Chapter Concerning the Day of
Gathering), we find these chilling words:

Say, O ye who are Jews; if you claim that you are favored of
Allah apart from all mankind, then long for death if you are
untruthful. (verse 6, Pickthal translation)

Here, the belief that the Jews were chosen by the Almighty as his covenant people, is challenged. The meaning of the phrase, "then long for death if you are untruthful" has two possible interpretations. In the first interpretation, these words are similar to the expression "on the pain of death, I assert that such as such is true." An oath is indicated. The other possible interpretation is more radical and implies that if the Jews are God's chosen people, then suffering and death await them. The source of such suffering and death is unclear. Either way, the implication is that the Jewish people can lose their status as God's covenant people because of their sin.

Surat al-Tawba (Arabic, Chapter of Repentance) notes:

> Fight those who do not believe in Allah, nor in the latter day, nor do they prohibit what Allah and his Messenger have prohibited, nor follow the religion of truth, out of those who have been given the Book, until they pay the tax [*jizya*] in acknowledgment of superiority, and they are in a state of subjection. (verse 29, Shakir translation)

In this verse, Muhammad tells the early Muslim communities to battle unbelievers, including the Jewish people, those who were given "the Book" (the Torah). Some may claim that the "fight" of verse 29 merely refers to theological debate and the discussion of political ideals. However, in this verse, the word *qatilu* (Arabic, physical struggle) is used.

Today, more moderate Muslims may not apply verses from the *Qur'an* in the manner described above, but radical fundamentalists consider these applications to be *valid and necessary in the 21st century*. Their thought process goes like this:

1) The Jewish people err in their fundamental beliefs.
2) This makes them enemies of both Allah and Muslims.
3) It follows that the modern Jewish State of Israel is an abomination to Allah and the entire Muslim world.

The idea that the Jewish people should have an independent political state in the midst of land that fundamentalists believe was given to Muslims by Allah, is nothing short of blasphemous, and must be opposed. Violent action is too often taught as *the* accepted method of opposition. The nation of Israel has become the embodiment of the unbelieving, condemned Jewish people, and making war against her is considered to be carrying out the judgements that

Allah decreed in the seventh century. True believers in the Islamic world teach that Muslims should rule over the Middle East and that lands, such as Israel, once ruled by Muslims, remain the property of Islam. These lands are termed *waqf*, that is, forever Muslim property through an inherent religious right.

The very next verse in the *Qur'an* states:

The Jews say: Ezra is the son of Allah, and Christians call the Messiah the son of Allah. That is a saying from their mouth. [In this] they . . . imitate what the unbelievers of old used to say. Allah's curse be on them: how they are deluded away from the truth. (*Surat al-Tawba*, verse 30, Shakir translation)

Both Jewish and Christian communities are portrayed as cursed by the Divine power for believing such falsehoods. Muslim fundamentalists take this condemnation to mean that the Jewish people are fundamentally flawed. We can not be certain that this is the message that Muhammad intended to convey. However, this verse can be, and is, interpreted in this way. Furthermore, I do not know of any Jewish community in history, that ever considered Ezra to be the son of the Almighty in the same way that Christians consider Yeshua (Jesus) to be the son of the Almighty. Thus, the historical accuracy of Muhammad's assertion cannot be established.

Surat al-Imran (Arabic, The Family of Imran) records these words:

. . . among them [the Jews] are some believers, but most of them are evil-livers. (verse 110, Pickthal translation; the Yusufali translation uses the phrase "perverted transgressors" in place of "evil-livers")

This is verse is attributed to the period after the Al-Badr battle (624), in which the Banu Qurayza were charged with breaking a political alliance with Muhammad. More mainstream Islam may have considered these "perverted transgressors" to refer to the Banu Qurayza tribe alone. Yet again, these words are cannon fodder for Muslim extremists who seek a religious rationale for their violence against Israel, which represents the modern embodiment of the Banu Qurayza. In the same sura (verse 78), Jews are accused of lying about Allah through their written works (possibly the Talmud, which was codified in the previous century). This is, perhaps, the first written denunciation of the Talmud in history.

Woe betide those that write the scriptures with their own hands and then declare: "this is from God" in order to gain some paltry end. Woeful shall be their fate, because of what their hands have written, because of what they did! (verses 78–79)

In *Surat al-Bayyinah* (Chapter Concerning the Proof), Muhammad decrees judgment upon the Jewish people and pagans, who refused to believe in him:

The unbelievers among the People of the Book and the pagans shall burn forever in the fire of hell. They are the vilest of creatures. (verse 7, Dawood translation)

One of the most revealing verses concerning Muslim relations with ancient Jewish communities is found in *Surat al-Tawba*:

When the sacred months are over [Muslim months of *Shawwal, Dhul-Qu'adah, Dhul-Hajjah* and *Muharram*], slay the idolaters wherever you find them. Arrest them, besiege them, and lie in ambush everywhere for them. If they repent and take to prayer and render the alms-levy, allow them to go their way. (verse 5, Dawood translation)

In this *sura*, Muhammad speaks against the Jewish tribes and a state of war is declared against those who would resist him. The chapter continues:

Believers, why is it that when you are told: "March in the cause of God," you linger slothfully in the land. . . . Whether unarmed or well equipped, march on and fight for the cause of God, with your wealth and with your persons. This will be best for you, if you but knew it. (verses 38 and 41, Dawood translation)

Some of Muhammad's early followers were not enthusiastic about warring. Hence, the *Qur'an* upbraids them and then encourages them to bear arms against those who resist Islam. A radical fundamentalist interpretation of these verses leads to the conclusion that this call to war is valid today. Furthermore, the enemies of Islam are the Jews, especially Israeli Jews, and the United States, as the supreme embodiment of the secular, non-Muslim world.

The Hadith

The *Hadith* (Arabic, saying) are a collection of teachings attributed to Muhammad, which are not found in the Qur'an. Some portions of the *Hadith* are noteworthy. An early Muslim leader, Abu Huraira, quoted one of Muhammad's teachings:

> The hour will not be established until you fight with the Jews, and the stone behind which a Jew will be hiding will say, O Muslim, there is a Jew hiding behind me, so kill him. (*Hadith, Jihad*, 177, Khan translation)

It is unclear if the above *hadith* was meant for one particular Jewish tribe in Medina, or the Jewish people in general. However, Palestinian terrorists have used it as religious epithet to support their violence against Israelis.

In another *hadith*, Aisha, one of Muhammad's wives, is quoted as saying:

> The messenger in his final days said, "Allah cursed the Jews and Christians because they took the graves of their prophets as places for praying." (*Hadith, Al-Janaa'iz*, 414, Khan translation)

This may refer to the ancient Jewish tradition of gathering for prayers at the burial sites of biblical figures and honored rabbis. In this *hadith*, this practice of both the Jewish and the Christian communities is censured. However, in Israel today, Muslims, as well as Jews and Christians, pray at the graves of biblical figures. The Cave of Machpelah, in Hebron, and Rachel's tomb, in Bethlehem, are two such sites of prayer.

Another *hadith*, given by Abu Musa, sheds more light on early Muslim thought about the Jewish people:

> The example of Muslims, Jews and Christians is like the example of a man who employed laborers to work for him from morning until night. They worked till midday and they

said, "We are not in need of your reward." So the man employed another batch and said to them, "Complete the rest of the day and yours will be the wages I had fixed [for the first batch]." They worked up till the time of the Asr prayer and said, "Whatever we have done is done for you." He employed another batch. They worked for the rest of the day till sunset, and they received the wages of the two former batches. (*Hadith, Awqat salah*, 533, Khan translation)

Here, both the first batch of workers (the Jews), and the second batch of workers (the Christians), stopped working for their employer, who represents the Almighty. Their rewards were bestowed upon the third group (the Muslims), who are seen as the true and faithful servants of God. Hence, this passage teaches that the Almighty's blessings for Jews and Christians have ceased.

The *Hadith* also recalls the murder of the Banu Qurayza tribe:

Some people [the Jews of Banu Qurayza] agreed to accept the verdict of Sad bin Muad. He [Sad] came riding on a donkey, and when he approached the Mosque, the Prophet [Muhammad] said, "Rise up [in respect] for the best among you," or he said, "Rise up [in respect] for your chief [judge]." Then the Prophet [Muhammad] said, "Sad, these people have agreed to accept your verdict." Sad said, "I judge that their warriors should be killed, and their children and women should be taken as captives." The Prophet [Muhammad] said, "You have given a judgment similar to Allah's judgment." (*Hadith, Ansaar*, 148, Khan translation)

Muhammad had appointed Sad to decide the tribe's fate following their alleged betrayal in 627. Sad decreed that death should come to all males above the age of puberty, and that slavery and/or forced conversion to Islam should be the lot of the other members of this tribe.

Muslim-Jewish Relations in the Middle Ages

During some periods, Muslim governments showed tolerance for the Jewish people living within their borders. For much of the 700-year history of *Al-Andalus*, the Jewish people dwelt in relative peace and security. The quality of life they experienced in Andalusian Spain was in marked contrast to the circumstances they encountered throughout the rest of the Muslim world.

Jewish life flourished under *Al-Andalus'* Umayyad governments. Great religious, philosophical, and scientific gains were made during this epoch. Some of the most notable personalities of the period were: the poet, Yehudah Halevi (d. 1145), the Torah scholar, Avraham Ibn Ezra (d. 1164), and the liturgist, Shlomo Ibn Gvirol (d. 1058). Additionally, the famous Torah scholar, the Rambam (Maimonides, d. 1204) was born in *Al-Andalus*. However, as a young man, he had to flee the country because of the intolerant policies of the Almohade ruling dynasty.

Under Umayyad domination, the Jewish communities had limited autonomy. However, they were able to freely practice their religion. One Jewish physician, Hasday Ibn Shaprut (d. 970) became an advisor to two successive caliphs. The Caliphate of Cordova, functioning until 1031, was a famous seat of Torah study and translation, as well as of philosophy, medicine, literature, mathematics, and earth science. However, with the coming of the Muslim fundamentalist Almoravide dynasty in 1055, intolerance reared its head. The ensuing Almohade rulers (from 1147) continued the policy of discrimination against the Jewish communities.

The "golden age" of *Al-Andalus* was relatively short-lived, and not characteristic of the typical experiences of Jewish people residing in Muslim lands. Some regions were welcoming; others were not as hospitable. The Jewish communities experienced ups and downs in their quality of life and societal status. Despite, any periods of tolerance, they were always considered a *dhimmi* population, subject to the whims of local Muslim rulers.

Chapter Four

THE FOMENTING FERVOR

To its credit, Islam teaches the acceptance of adherents to the faith from any background, race, or nationality. Yet, in actuality, religious tolerance has been something that the Muslim world, in general, knows very little about. Stories related by Christians in Indonesia, Malaysia, and Saudi Arabia tell of much suffering at the hand of Muslim majorities.

The Sudan, a country in which the majority of its inhabitants are Muslim, experienced a war between its Muslim population in the north, and its African Christian and animist populations in the south. The African Christians and animists were severely decimated. It is simplistic to say that religion was the only factor in this war. There were political, economic, and racial causes as well. Yet, since Christians and pagans fought against Muslims, the role of religion was fundamental in the formation of this twenty five-year old conflict, in which over 500,000 Sudanese lost their lives.

In the in late 1970s and early 1980s, the Palestine Liberation Organization (PLO), now known by its more sterile name, the Palestinian Authority, persecuted the Lebanese Maronites, a Christian community. During that same time, the Muslim-dominated PLO occupied southern Lebanon, decimating many Christian communities. Many Christians left Lebanon permanently because their lives were in danger.

When the Israeli Army went into southern Lebanon in 1982 as part of *mivtza shalom le galil,* or Operation *Sheleg* (Hebrew acronym, Peace for the Galilee), a number of Israeli military officers were hoisted in the air by Lebanese Christian villagers during a celebration. A colonel in the Israeli Defense Forces, told me about the warm, thankful welcome he received upon arriving in southern Lebanon, after the unit under his command routed the PLO from the area.

It has been sad to see so many Palestinian Christians leave Bethlehem, an area governed by the PA. They often cite economic hardship as their main reason for departure. However, we cannot minimize the intimidating effect that Muslim majority has upon the minority Christian community. Arab Christians keep a close eye on the day-to-day attitudes of the PA. A Christian friend from Bethlehem told me that he was not too worried about PA persecution because he participated in activities that help clothe and feed poor Muslims in that area. Though his actions were laudable, he might not feel as safe if his Western source of clothes and food dried up.

Some Palestinian Christians boldly speak out against alleged civil liberty violations at the hands of the Israelis. Yet, they will not raise their voices to protest the routine human rights abuses committed by the Palestinian Authority. Palestinians freely denounce the Israeli government. Their critical remarks are often quoted in the Israeli press and international media. However, the same people will utter not a word against Yassir Arafat, and the known corruption in his government. Why don't they speak out? The answer is that they are concerned about retribution from the PA security forces.

In 2000, I participated in a seminar with another speaker, a Palestinian Christian. He publicly blasted Israel, accusing my nation of many wrongs, but offered no proof of his assertions. Speaking after him, I outlined the recent activities of the Palestinian Authority, offering quotes from prominent PA officials and proofs of their incitements to violence. Additionally, I outlined our historical hope for peace, and provided specific data detailing Israel's casualties to let the audience know that my nation has indeed suffered because of Palestinian terror. The audience of more than four hundred people reacted with overwhelming sympathy for Israel's situation vis-à-vis the Palestinian Authority.

My fellow speaker was well aware of the quality of the PA's leadership, yet his stance made it clear that he could not address their lack of integrity without suffering retribution. If a real passion for human rights existed in his community, people would speak against their government.

There is a growing chasm between Palestinian Muslims and Palestinian Christians. I attended a private lecture given by Mr. Anwar ibn Najeeb, a Palestinian Christian and lifelong resident of the Middle East. The speaker shared his thoughts about the future of his people, Arab Christians, in a Muslim dominated society. First, he corrected the teaching that says the word *Islam* means "peace." He stated:

Islam means submission, slave submission to Allah. *Salam* is
the Arabic word for *peace*, not *Islam*.[1]

He proceeded to explain how verses in the *Qur'an* are interpreted
by fundamentalist Muslims to validate militant action against the
Western world. In the minds of the extremists, Israel and the United
States represent the modern embodiment of the "People of the Book."

Muslims tend to think of the West as Christian, and of this
present conflict as Islam verses Christianity. . . . Though early
in his career Muhammad recited verses that were kind to
non-Muslims, later in his life, his language changed.[2]

It was heartening to hear an educated Palestinian Christian ex-
press great concern about the fact that his people will become the
subjects of increased discrimination by the neighboring Muslim
world, *not by Israelis.*

As fundamentalist fervor grows in Muslim countries around the
world, not just in the Palestinian territories, minority groups are
suffering increased oppression. Militant Islam continues to grow
strong in Egypt, Libya, Algeria, the Sudan, Somalia, Lebanon, Syria,
Afghanistan, Iran, Indonesia, Malaysia, and South Africa. Iraq
thrives on its brand of political extremism. In Nigeria, the Christian
population, approximately one half of the people, is threatened by
Muslim intolerance, essentially the other half of the population.

The Fundamentalist Mindset

Charles Selengut, Professor of Religious Studies at Drew University,
informs us that fundamentalists see non-Muslims as *harbi* (Arabic,
outsiders who need to submit to Islam). He noted:

The world, in the [fundamentalist] Muslim view, is divided
between *Islam* and *war*, and the devout Muslim believer must
answer the call of jihad to advance Allah's message for all hu-
mankind. . . . The faithful Muslim's duty is to engage in religious struggle, jihad, to transform the *Dar al-Harb* (Arabic,
non-Muslim lands) into *Dar Al-Islam* (Arabic, Muslim
lands) into lands governed by Muslim law . . . the call to jihad
remains a potent force in Islamic doctrine and religious
imagination.[3]

Dr. Selengut provided additional insight into a complex issue:

The world today, as was the world that faced Mohammed, is a world of *Jahiliya*, barbarism and immorality, and a Muslim must not acquiesce or compromise in any way with this type of society. Modernity and Islam are entirely incompatible, And a Muslim must do everything, including mounting a militant jihad, to construct a Muslim society where Muslims can be free of the dangers of *Jahiliyah*. *Jahiliyah* is the sworn enemy of Islam.[4]

Many followers of Muhammad look at current events through these lenses. Thus, we can understand why there is such a great reluctance on the part of Muslims to participate in military action against their co-religionists. This is why Saudi government may despise Osama bin Laden and *Al-Qa'eda*, and speak out against them, but they will not lift a finger to help the United States-led efforts to destroy him and his evil network.

Although Saddam Hussein warred against Iran and Kuwait, which are both Muslim countries, these conflicts should be viewed as political struggles for control within the house of Islam. In the Gulf War, his maniacal thirst for power turned some Muslim nations, even fascist ones such as Syria, against Iraq. The 1980s war between Iraq and Iran pitted Arabs (Iraqis) against Indo-Europeans (Iranians). The conflict was not a religious one, although Iran, couched its war propaganda in religious terms. Saddam's quest for power, versus a new Iranian government's desire for military superiority over their Iraqi-strongman neighbor, was the issue in this situation.

Wars between Muslim nations have been numerous. Religious fervor is tapped to gain popular support. Yet, the essence of such wars is *not* necessarily religious. When Jordan's King Hussein fought the PLO in the 1970s, it was one Muslim army against another. However, religion was not the issue. Rather, it was the PLO's influence and the threat they posed to social stability within Jordan. When Egypt and Yemen battled in the 1960s, the issue was politics, not religion.

However, when a non-Muslim nation comes against a Muslim nation, the issue of religion is frequently raised. Israel's struggle to exist is testified to by four official wars, plus ongoing wars of attrition. Her Arab neighbors have often justified their continual campaigns against the Jewish state by religious reasoning. Muslim nations view Israelis as "infidels," occupying land that according to Islamic teaching, cannot belong to unbelievers.

Sadly, the Arab peoples of the Middle East have not really known what it is like to live in a free democracy. I am not aware of any Arab nation, even if it has elections, that has a democratic system like the United States. Goals that have fueled America's existence—life, liberty, and the pursuit of happiness—have never been priorities in the Arab world. As Arab nations overall have few civil liberties, it is hypocritical for them to censure Israel for alleged human rights violations. Israel is not accepted by most Muslim nations *precisely because Israel is not a Muslim nation.*

Sensitivities Inflamed

Radical Muslim religious fervor encourages intolerance and hatred. In fundamentalist rhetoric, the United States has been referred to as "the big satan," and Israel has been called "the little satan." From the Gaza Strip to Iran, these epithets have been used.

Theologically speaking, fundamentalist Islam provides the motivation and justification for extremist actions for people who consider themselves disenfranchised by the Western world. One can attempt to rationalize any deed from the pages of the Jewish and Christian Bible. The same idea holds true in the Muslim world, vis-à-vis the Qur'an. Muslim Extremists will search the writings of the *Qur'an* for reasons to perpetrate violence against Western targets.

Furthermore, one should not underestimate the influence of a deeply rooted anger, which is present in the hearts of many radical fundamentalists. This animosity is widespread, and aimed at Westerners, who are seen as having gained their wealth by oppressing Muslim nations. Some of this anger is vented at the leadership of Muslim governments such as Saudi Arabia, Oman, Abu Dhabi and Bahrain, which have become extremely wealthy through oil sales to the Western world. Anger about low economic status seethes and overflows in two directions: toward the Western world and toward wealthy pro-Western Muslim governments. Radical fundamentalists view foreign economic influence as oppressive and a betrayal of the Muslim world and of Islam itself. Therefore, this Western influence is worthy of opposition.

In some sense, this was Saddam Hussein's motivation when he targeted Saudi Arabia during the Gulf War. He saw the Saudis as traitorous to the true Muslim cause; yet, this was probably a secondary reason for his actions. Perhaps, the greatest motivating factor for his assault was Saudi opposition to his designs on the Kuwaiti oil industry and his intention of becoming the Middle East's most powerful ruler.

One might think that when Arab nations became politically independent, their anger against the Western would have abated. However, this has not happened. As former Israeli Prime Minister Binyamin Netanyahu wrote:

> Nor has political independence allayed Arab resentment and frustration: rather, it has provided a more effective means for expressing both–in the form of Pan-Arab nationalist and immoderate Islamic governments claiming to be reviving the Arab people and returning it to the justly deserved glory of which the West has deprived it.[5]

Some American Muslims have expressed this same resentment and frustration, lashing out at Israel as the cause of their feelings. On October 31, 2001, on an American television broadcast from Washington D.C., the New Black Panther Party hosted a sparsely attended public forum at which their chief officer intimated that Israel's security forces carried out the 1998 bombing of the American Embassy in Kenya. Over two hundred people were murdered, and his proof of Israeli involvement was this statement:

> We don't believe that a Muslim would carry out an act in which African people would be killed.[6]

This officer then passed out a document that supposedly proved Israeli involvement in the bombing. He somewhat hesitatingly admitted that he had never personally read the document and therefore, could not comment upon it. His accusations against Israel furthers the public stereotype, particularly to African Americans and other minority communities, of my country being the "bad bully boy" of the Middle East. The American intelligence community never made such a connection, nor did they ever even consider the New Black Panther Party's naïve assertion. Israel sent a rescue team to help save Kenyan and American victims. The governments of Kenya and the United States publicly thanked Israel for their assistance in a time of need. Four bin Laden associates were convicted for the embassy attack after a trial in an American court. Another suspect, with ties to *Al-Qa'eda*, was arrested on December 10, 2001 for having connections to this heinous act of terrorism.

Public accusations, such as the one described above, are spawned because of anti-Semitic attitudes. Hopefully, the average American citizen will be able to make the distinction between these types of unfounded charges and the truth. The overwhelming majority of African Americans, with whom I have spoken about these issues, have acknowledged that Israel represents the Middle East's only democracy, and is therefore deserving of American support.

The recent immigration of Ethiopian Jews to Israel, a heartrending story of the Israeli government's attempt to save a doomed population, has opened many African American eyes. When I taught college in Israel, my heart broke as I listened to the stories my Ethiopian Jewish students told about how their families came to Israel. Almost all were penniless, and had members of their family die of starvation or disease along the way. Many marched hundreds of miles to the nearest Israeli airlift site. In 1985, I lectured on the Ethiopian Jewish immigration at an NAACP (National Association for the Advancement of Colored People) meeting in the Midwest. The stories I told of these immigrations brought tears to some eyes, and evoked sympathy for Israel's aim to be a refuge for all Jews, black-skinned or white-skinned, *Ashkenazi* or *Sephardi* (Hebrew for European and Oriental Jewry, respectively).

Some groundless accusations in America against Israel began as hoaxes, which started shortly after the September 11 attacks. These lies, originating in the Middle East, blamed Israel for the destruction of the World Trade Center. Bryan Curtis documents the flow of this slander in his Internet article, "Four Thousand Jews, One Lie," an excellent piece that describes how such stories began and were disseminated to the American public.[7]

I have studied and worked with Muslims who realize that Israel has a right to exist as an independent Jewish state. They are able to separate their religious convictions from their political beliefs. Two such acquaintances commented on how hypocritical it is for their countries to routinely accuse Israel of human rights violations, when in their lands, Libya and Somalia, human rights do not exist. In his article, "Memo to American Muslims," Dr. Khan, a Muslim professor of International Studies at Adrian College, reasons with his co-religionists:

Muslims have been practicing hypocrisy on a grand scale. They protest against the discriminatory practices of Israel, but are silent against the discriminatory practices in Muslim states. . . . I must remind you that Israel treats its one million Arab citizens with greater respect and dignity than most Arab nations treat their own citizens. Have we ever demanded international intervention or retribution against Saddam [Hussein] for gassing Kurds . . . against Saudis for abusing the Shi'ites [a wing of Islam], against Syria for the massacre at Hama? We condemn Israel, not because we care for rights and lives of the Palestinians—we don't. We condemn Israel because we hate *them*. Muslims love to live in the United States, but we also love to hate it. Many openly claim that the United States is a terrorist state, yet their presence here is testimony that they would rather live here than anywhere else. . . . It is time that we acknowledge that the freedoms we enjoy in America are more desirable to us than superficial solidarity with the Muslim world. If you disagree, then prove it by packing your bags and going to whichever Muslim country you identify with. . . . It is time that we faced these hypocritical practices and struggled to transcend them. It is time that American Muslim leaders fought to purify their own lot.[8]

A Beirut Newspaper, *The Daily Star*, reported:

Recent years have seen Lebanon's leadership blame Israel for everything from a riot at a concert to the assassination of judges. The facts come out, but no one seems to learn the lesson . . . the habit of instinctively attributing mishaps to Israel makes all branches of the Lebanese state look even more unprofessional than they are. . . . The [Lebanese] leadership therefore does itself no favors when senior figures pontificate on topics about which they know little or nothing.[9]

The Arab journalist who wrote this article has seen how Israel has been routinely blamed for all of Lebanon's woes, and considers this knee-jerk reaction to be unfounded. Kuwaiti professor Shafeeq Ghabra confronted this mindset with these words:

The Lebanese civil war was not an American creation; neither was the Iran-Iraq war, neither was bin Laden. These are our [Arab and Muslim] creations. We need to look inside. We cannot be in this blame-others mode forever.[10]

Muslim moderate voices of reason must speak out. The leader of Italy's Muslim community, Imam Abdul Hadi Palazzi, voiced a refreshing opinion when he *opposed* a call to *jihad* against Israel. He cited his belief that Israel should not have to give up sovereignty as long as Muslim sites are respectfully maintained. Charles Selengut and Yigal Carmon comment upon the wing of more modern Muslims who adjust their hermeneutics according to political reality, resulting in their ability to theologically accept the presence of non-Muslims.[11]

Even so, the ability to accept non-Muslims does not always lead to a peaceful solution of the problems. For example, The Democratic Front for the Liberation of Palestine (DFLP), for many years, under the direction of George Habash, is a murderous, anti-Semitic organization, which has a pro-Communist ideology. Habash comes from an ethnically Arab Christian background and defends his right to murder Jews solely upon modern secular political ideology.

Khaled Muhammad Batrafi, in the London daily *Al-Hayat* (Arabic, life), responded to the call to destroy Israel in an article outlining a conversation with a Muslim friend; they argued about whether the *Qur'an* adjures Muslims to annihilate the "People of the Book" (Jews and Christians). His friend stated:

> The teacher at the [local] mosque called for the death and annihilation of Christians and Jews; he called to make their children orphans and their wives widows.[12]

Batrafi attempted to convince his acquaintance of fallacy of his position. Their discussion centered on proper interpretation of the *Qur'an*, with his friend stating, "Do you support Christians and Jews? If so, the words of Allah apply to you. Whoever supports them, belongs to them." Batrafi then argued that Muhammad taught Muslims not to fight with Christians and Jews, but to dialogue with them. His friend responded by saying that the Jews of Medina, as recorded in the *Qur'an*, were hostile to Muslims, and therefore, Jews today deserve the same punishment meted out by Muhammad in the seventh century.

Batrafi's column portrays the modern-day dilemma that many Muslims experience. How should the *Qur'an* be interpreted in regard to its teachings about Christians and Jews? Obviously, Batrafi's friend held a specific interpretation, one that is gaining great ground in the fundamentalist movement today. The more rational view of Mr. Batrafi is also extant in the Muslim world. Each looks at the *Qur'an*'s teachings about relations with the *ahm al-kitab* (Arabic, people of the Book) in fundamentally different fashions.

The problem is that radical fundamentalists have not allowed the history of Muhammad's relations with the tribes of Medina to be put to rest. Moderates rationalize that Muhammad's words and actions involved the *historical* situation of some fourteen and a half centuries ago, and that the condemnations pronounced against these Jewish communities are not carried over today. Moderate Muslims may have political problems with the existence of Israel as a country, but not all of them are inspired to war against the Jewish state.

Voices of Palestinian Fundamentalism

In a sermon on October 13, 2000, Ahmad Abu Halabiya, appointed by the Palestinian Authority to its Religious Edicts Council, stated:

> Wherever you are, kill those Jews and those Americans who are like them, and those who stand by them; they are all in one trench, against the Arabs and the Muslims . . . even if an agreement on Gaza is signed, we shall not forget Haifa, Akko, the Galilee and Yafo, the Triangle and the Negev, and the rest of our cities and villages. . . . We will not give up a single grain of soil . . . from Haifa and Yafo, and Akko and Petah Tikva, and Ashkelon, and all the land, and Gaza and the West Bank.[13]

PA religious authorities have no sympathy for the United States' recent travails. On October 11, 2001, CNN News reported on a poll taken in the PA territories, which affirmed that the majority of Palestinians opposed American-led strikes in Afghanistan. It was also reported that one in four Palestinians polled believed that the September 11 attacks were consistent with their interpretation of Muslim law. The PA, under Mr. Arafat's direction, appointed Sheikh Ikrimah Sabri as *mufti* (Arabic, supreme head cleric) of the Palestinian people. The Middle Eastern Media and Research Institute (MEMRI) is a watchdog group that monitors the speeches and writings of the Arab world. On September 28, 2001, it reported that, Sheikh Sabri publicly urged his listeners, at the *Al-Aksa* Mosque in Jerusalem, to rally against the emerging American-led coalition against terrorism and Operation Enduring Freedom.

Abu Halabiya later remarked in a public sermon in Gaza:

The Jews are the allies of the Christians, and the Christians are the allies of the Jews, despite the enmity that exists between them . . . all of them are in agreement against the monotheists [Muslim world] . . . that is, they are in agreement against you, O Muslims. . . . Our people must unite . . . and receive armaments from the Palestinian leadership, to confront the Jews . . . have no mercy on the Jews, no matter where they are, in any country. Fight them . . . wherever you meet them, kill them.[14]

In a sermon at Jerusalem's *Al-Aksa* Mosque, Muslim cleric Sheik Abu Sneina declared:

Muslim Palestine is one and cannot be divided. There is no difference between Haifa and Nablus, Lod and Ramallah, Jerusalem and Nazareth or Gaza and Ashkelon. Palestine is *Wakf* land that belongs to Muslims throughout the world and no one has the right to give it up or to forsake [it]. Whoever does this is a traitor to the trust and is nothing but a criminal [according to Abu Sneina's interpretation of Muslim law] whose end shall be in hell.[15]

Dr. Abu Halabiya continued his contemptuous discourse:

No one, no Arab, Palestinian or Muslim is allowed to forgo one grain of soil of the land of Palestine, Jerusalem and Al-Aksa [Temple Mount in Jerusalem] . . . whoever forgoes even one grain of soil will be punished for his sin, for the sins of all Palestinians, for the sins of all Arabs and for all of the Muslims' sins forever and ever . . . Allah decreed on us in this lifetime to humiliate the Jews sooner or later . . . I swear by Allah, the Jews are Islam's enemies in this lifetime.[16]

He offered even more incitement to violence and religious martyrdom by stating:

Allah has purchased from the believers their persons and their property in return for the promise that they shall have paradise, for they fight in the cause of Allah, and they slay the enemy and are slain. This is a promise that Allah has made incumbent upon Himself, as set out in the Torah, and Gospel and the Qur'an.[17]

And:

Allah has called upon us not to ally with the Jews or the Christians, not to like them, not to become their partners, not to support them, and not to sign agreements with them. And he who does that is one of them! As Allah said, "O you who believe do not take the Jews and Christians as allies . . . they are against you, O Muslims!" . . . They [Jews] are the terrorists. They are the ones who must be butchered and killed, as Allah said, "Fight them." Allah will torture them at your hands, and will humiliate them and will help you to overcome them. . . . all of them [Jews and Christians] are in agreement against the monotheists [Muslims], against those who say, "There is no God but Allah and Muhammad is his messenger"; that is, they are against you, O Muslims.[18]

Dr. Halabiya spoke these words on Palestinian television, where he had considerable influence over his audience. Palestinian television is controlled by the PA, which should raise serious doubts about the sincerity of Palestinian desires to live in peace with Israel and to battle terrorism. The theme of continual, violent *jihad* against the Jews (Israelis, in modern terms) is clearly set forth in Abu Halabiya's speech.

This type of television programming reveals the hypocrisy of the PA. Palestinian television plays on Muslim religious sentiments to incite the general population against Israel. Note these words from a broadcast on August 11, 2001:

How can we be happy today, and how can we smile while Jerusalem is being trampled, while Jerusalem is in danger and on the brink of the establishment of the third [Jewish] Temple? That is what they [Israelis] are trying to do today. They want to establish the Temple on the land of Al-Aksa and Jerusalem . . . with the blessing of the entire government of Israel and the government of all the Jews. With the establishment of the Temple will be the beginning of the destruction of the Al-Aksa Mosque and the building of the Temple on top of its ruins.[19]

The message that Israel intends to destroy Muslim religious sites is an outright lie. But the ability of Palestinians to think rationally about these issues is next to impossible when such slander is continually spread on the airwaves.

Again, on August 11, 2001, Palestinian television broadcasted these charged remarks:

> Oh our Arab brothers . . . oh our Muslim brothers . . . don't leave the Palestinians alone in war against the Jews. . . . Jerusalem, Palestine and Al-Aksa . . . will remain the center of the battle of truth and falsehood between the Jews and non-Jews. . . . Palestine . . . causes the Jews sleeplessness at night, causes sleeplessness to Allah's enemies [which are presumably the Jews] throughout the world. . . . Jerusalem is a symbol of the Muslim's unity and it is a symbol to their strength and to the Muslim people's jihad forever.[20]

These are among the most influential religious voices within the Palestinian world. Their rhetoric reflects a religious hermeneutic that leads to the hatred of Israelis (and all Jews).

Abu Halabiya's rhetoric reflects the use of this hermeneutic:

> Allah has purchased from the believers their persons and their property in return for the promise that they shall have paradise, for they fight in the cause of Allah, and they slay the enemy and are slain. This is a promise that Allah has made incumbent upon Himself, as set out in the Torah, and Gospel and the Qur'an.[21]

He continued, quoting from the Qur'ran:

> Allah has called upon us not to ally with the Jews or the Christians, not to like them, not to become their partners, not to support them, and not to sign agreements with them. And he who does that is one of them! As Allah said, "O you who believe, do not take the Jews and Christians as allies . . . they are against you, O Muslims!"[22]

> They [Jews] are the terrorists. They are the ones who must be butchered and killed, as Allah said, "Fight them. Allah will

torture them at your hands, and will humiliate them and will help you to overcome them."[23]

Abu Halabiya summarized his militant, fundamentalist perspective in these words:

> ... all of them [Jews and Christians] are in agreement against the monotheists [Muslims], against those who say, "There is no God but Allah and Muhammad is his messenger"; that is, they are against you, O Muslims.[24]

Again, these statements, influencing an entire generation, were broadcast by Palestinian Television. When Qur'anic teachings concerning the Jewish and Christian world are taken out of their historical context and applied to the 21st century, Islam becomes fertile ground for hate groups to use religious beliefs to justify murder.

Encouraging Religious Martyrdom

On Friday, August 17, 2001, the Palestinian Broadcasting Authority televised a sermon by Sheik Isma'il Al-Ghadwan from Gaza. He taught:

> It is the duty of the Islamic nation to open the gates of jihad, where its strength and honor lie. . . . Sa'ad bin Abi Waqqas tells the story of Abdallah bin Jash, who wished to launch a jihad and never come back. . . . He was hoping to get [to Paradise] early in order to meet the Prophet when he dies. . . . [Abdallah bin Jash] said on the eve of the battle of Uhud: "O Allah, bring me tomorrow an enraged and furious man and I will fight him for your sake, and he will fight me, overcome me, and chop off my ear and nose. . . . When the enemies of Allah, the Jews, may Allah curse them, mutilate the bodies and chop off organs, these organs will serve as evidence for our sons and brothers for whom Paradise . . . is a place of refuge. Oh believing brothers, we do not feel a loss [over a martyr]. . . . The martyr, if he meets Allah, is forgiven with the first drop of blood; he is saved from the torments of the grave; he sees his place in Paradise; he is saved from the Great Horror of the day of judgment; he is given

seventy two black-eyed women; he vouches for seventy of his family to be accepted to Paradise; he is crowned with the crown of glory."[25]

The message to Muslim youths and families is that this is the religious ideal for which strive—to be a *shahid* (religious martyr). In his theological justification of martyrdom and murder, Sheik Al-Gadwan invokes a story from the Battle of Uhud, which took place during the early days of Islam. He attempts to convince young men to take that historical situation and apply it to modern times. Its message for today is that spilling blood in martyrdom is a great act. This teaching would be akin to modern Americans teaching their youth that because the British opposed your ancestors in the Revolutionary War, they oppose you today, and therefore, it is meritorious to murder British citizens. In fact, such action is the American ideal for any young man seeking to serve his country and his God.

On August 3, 2001 Sheik Ibrahim Mahdi commented at Sheik 'Ijlin Mosque in Gaza:

A young man said to me, "I am fourteen years old and I have four years left before I blow myself up amongst the Jews." I said to him, "Oh son, I ask Allah to give you and myself martyrdom." . . . We must all seek a role in the jihad and the battle. . . . The Quran is very clear on this: the greatest enemies of the Islamic nation are the Jews, may Allah fight them . . . . All spears should be directed at the Jews, at the enemies of Allah, the nation that was cursed in Allah's book; Allah has described them as apes and pigs, calf-worshippers, idol-worshippers . . . whoever can fight against them with his weapons, should go out; whoever can fight with a machine gun . . . with a sword or knife . . . with his hands . . . should go out. This is our destiny. The people who are most hostile toward the believers are the Jews and the polytheists . . . nothing will deter them except for us detonating ourselves in their midst. They have nuclear power, but we have the power of the belief in Allah. . . . The prophet Muhammad said: "The Jews will fight you, and Allah will establish you as rulers over them . . . " We blow them up in Hadera . . . in Tel Aviv and in Netanya, and in this way Allah establishes us as ruler over these gangs of vagabonds.[26]

This sheik encouraged his followers to commit child martyr-dom, and used events from the time of Muhammad to justify his murderous teachings. His hermeneutics reflect his one political goal: destroying the nation of Israel.

Former Israeli Prime Minister, Golda Meir, a mother herself, is known to have remarked, "When Arab mothers love their children more than they hate us, there can be peace." The extremist Muslim teaching that any adherent of their faith can have immediate en-trance into paradise by becoming a *shahid* contributes to the prac-tice of child martyrdom. Since all Israelis, and now Americans, are fingered as permitted targets of Islamic martyrs, young Muslims will be encouraged to freely murder both of our peoples. Entire states, such as Iran, Syria, and Iraq, are promoting this type of martyrdom. In these countries, as well as in areas controlled by militant Islamic terror organizations, the role of the *shahid* is glorified This *is* reality in the Middle East, though the great majority of Muslims in the United States may not accept this teaching.

Chapter Five

ISRAEL'S STRUGGLE AGAINST TERRORISM

As a student in 1972, I loved to watch sporting events. The Olympics fascinated me. It was thrilling to see athletes from all around the world giving their best to be international champions. The 1972 Munich Olympics held special meaning for Israel. It was the first time the games were held in Germany since 1936, when they took place in Berlin during the Nazi regime. I recalled that America's Jewish Olympians had not been allowed to participate, a last minute decision that further made the Berlin Olympics painful for my people.

Israel had mixed feelings about our team traveling to Germany. Some Israelis were enthusiastic, thinking the world had changed enough so that we could now safely send athletes to the land that was responsible for the murder of six million of our kinsmen. Our athletes would be able to compete on an equal footing with the athletes of other nations. A few Israelis were not as positive about our part in the games. They recalled our great sufferings in Germany—so much so, that for them, the idea of sending a team to the Olympics in Germany was a desecration of our painful history, twenty-seven years earlier.

In the end, Israel sent a team. The shocking events that occurred at those games are unforgettable. International terrorism, organized and financed by the "Black September" group of the PLO, under the direction of Yassir Arafat, was thrust into worldview through television. My parents and I sat at home, stunned, watching news reports about this heinous crime. I distinctly remember the hooded murderer, standing on the parapet of the Israeli team's dormitory, peering out at the world. Again, Jewish people were victims, in a country where we had already experienced untold suffering. This time, the crimes were not perpetrated by Germans, but by Arab terrorists, associated with Yassir Arafat.

On September 11, 2001, I was riveted to the television once again, watching the tragic events of that day unfold. In the evening, I saw news footage of large numbers of Palestinians celebrating the day's events. Later, it was reported that Yassir Arafat had denounced the attacks, denying any complicity in the evil acts.

However, the philosophical connection between the PLO's past activities and *Al-Qa'eda*'s current methodology is clear. Both groups believe that murder is an acceptable means of accomplishing their greater goals. Mr. Arafat *is* partially responsible for the September 11 tragedy. From the 1960s until now, his organization has vigorously promoted international terrorism. The PLO was a political trendsetter in radical Middle Eastern politics. Therefore, many Israelis do not believe that there is an ounce of integrity in Mr. Arafat's denial of involvement in the events of September 11. While he did not hire or train the *Al-Qa'eda* terrorists, he and his organization have trained and prepared many other participants in anti-Western terror.

Yassir Arafat's Terrorist History

After watching Mr. Arafat for the past thirty years, I was outraged at the image he presented to the world that day. Initially, his denial may have seemed fitting. However, the sight of those Palestinian celebrations made me wonder why Mr. Arafat denounced something that made his own people rejoice. I do not accuse all Palestinians of such inhumanity. I am sure that some of them experienced sorrow and shock over the tragedy. Yet, the images of cheering, celebrating Palestinians in places such as Nablus and East Jerusalem did not lie. These pictures demonstrated the fact that Palestinians are very comfortable with the use of violence and terrorism as a political expression. The Palestinian throngs were revealing their true wishes for the United States.

I have a photo in which a Palestinian youth is being hoisted upon the shoulders of an adult after the September 11 attacks. Armed with what looks like an AK-47 assault rifle, and wearing an American NFL football jersey, the youth is demonstrating in favor of the destruction of American lives! This photo reminds me of a story, told to me by my cousin, who studied at Wayne State University in the late 1960s. She had an Arab classmate, a foreign student, who seemed to be a decent, sympathetic human being. One day he stood up in class and announced, "I want to learn all I can about this country, and then bring it down."

Similarly, in spite of Mr. Arafat's denials, the actions of some of his people speak loudly. In an attempt to present a positive image of himself and the PA to the Western world, he denies his involvement in the events of September 11. The Palestine Authority's chairman did not want the world to recall his bloody past—a past in which he used international terrorism as a weapon. He endeavored to separate himself from Osama bin Laden and *Al-Qa'eda*.

Yassir Arafat's previous actions paved the way for the September 11 tragedy. He helped build the Palestine Liberation Organization. Israel understands that the name change to the Palestinian Authority is merely cosmetic. Under Mr. Arafat's leadership, the PLO was responsible for the 1972 Munich Olympics murders. It was also responsible for the hijacking of numerous airplanes and sea vessels, including the Achille Lauro in 1985, in which an American citizen was murdered. The hijacking of an Air France flight, which resulted in the 1976 Entebbe Airport hostage crisis, and the deaths of Israelis and Ugandans, was also the brainchild of the PLO. Mr. Arafat and his organization were responsible for the destabilization of southern Lebanon in the late 1970s and early 1980s. The PLO wreaked havoc among Lebanon's Christian population.

The PLO's destabilizing influence was not welcome in the Kingdom of Jordan. In 1970, the late King Hussein fought a short war against the PLO, successfully driving them out of his country. It is also important to remember that Mr. Arafat and the PLO helped Saddam Hussein intimidate the Kuwaitis in the Gulf War. Mr. Arafat's siding with Saddam Hussein was an overt act of aggression against Western democracy, against the United States, and against Israel' security.

After the 1990–1991 Gulf War, Mr. Arafat attempted to change his international image. To some extent, he succeeded. In the eyes of many, he was transformed from the world's best-known terrorist to a Nobel Prize winning peacemaker. Many in the international media were enamored with this new Arafat. He had now become a sympathetic and understanding man, someone who appeared to accept Israel's right to exist. What a drastic turnaround! Or was it?

From September 2000 to August 2001, Mr. Arafat's *Tanzim* militia soldiers killed some sixty-one Israelis. In 1983, they were established as his quasi-military force. Personal loyalty to Arafat was a prerequisite for participation in this militia. The *Tanzim* have been active in starting riots and carrying out armed attacks on Israeli

civilians. According to the Israel Defense Forces (IDF), they participated in the September 1996 Western Wall Tunnel riots and in the
May 2000 Nakba riots. They are also involved in the current *intifada*.
They distributed weapons, which were meant to be used against Israelis. They organized violent demonstrations and met with *Hamas*
leaders, advising them to agitate against Israel.[1] Mr. Arafat made no
effort to curtail any of these activities. Instead, he has used the
Tanzim militia to achieve goals that would have been impossible
through peaceful political negotiations.

On October 30, 2001, the Israel Broadcasting Authority reported
that a *Fatah* operative (or operatives) planted a bomb in the home of
an Israeli Naval officer in the city of Ra'anana.[2] Mr. Arafat's influence
is greatest in the *Fatah* wing of the PLO. After a spate of attacks
against Israel in the winter of 2001, President Bush rightly declared
Fatah to be a terrorist organization on March 22, 2002. Mr. Arafat has
enough power to prevent this group of his closest associates from
committing terrorist acts against Israel, but he has consistently refused
to use it. Hence, we cannot believe that he is serious about his commit-
ment to battle terrorism.

More terrorism has emanated from the PA since the Oslo Accords were signed than during all the six tumultuous years of the
first *intifada*. These facts demonstrate that there has not been a turnaround in attitudes and actions, but rather a continuation of Mr.
Arafat's earlier policies. He claims that he is serving the principles of
political independence and freedom. Israelis who have closely followed his actions since 1993 do not believe his assertions, regardless
of the face he presents to the Western world. Mr. Arafat's messages
in Arabic, to his own people, do not match his English rhetoric. His
public image and that of today's PA as peace-loving seekers of liberty match neither his messages nor his actions. I have no affection
for war. I will always back political efforts to avoid entering armed
conflict. However, Israel's current security situation is now out of
control.

After the PLO experienced initial successes in their use of international terror, other global organizations such as the German
Bader-Meinhof Gang, and the Italian and Japanese Red Brigades
adapted the PLO's methods. Additional organizations, including the
Popular Front for the Liberation of Palestine (PFLP), and later, the
Islamic *Jihad* and *Hamas*, developed political philosophies and
strategies similar to those used earlier by Mr. Arafat and the PLO.

The PLO was not the only organization that pioneered the use of terrorism. Certainly, a finger of blame can be pointed at others. However, in the late 20th century, the PLO was a major player in the spread of an ideology that encourages cold-blooded murder to achieve political goals.

Child Martyrdom as a Political Weapon

"Moderate," non-fundamentalist, Nobel Prize winner, Yassir Arafat, has never censured the practice of child martyrdom in PA territories, although he has the power to do so. His silence implies a recognition of the validity of this disgraceful act. Arafat has used child martyrdom as a political weapon against Israel. Interestingly, at the time this book went to press, his own daughter was comfortably living abroad, and had no plans to strap bombs to her body to murder Israelis.

During my military service, I witnessed the brutal phenomenon of using children as human shields. In the Gaza Strip, it was common for youths in their late teens to early twenties to begin riots while holding children in front of them. If the child suffered injury or death, the Israeli soldier was typically blamed. Violent things happened quickly because of the vicious, raucous mob mentality, which was fueled by hatred and religious fervor. Arab rioters quickly filled the air with bricks, iron bars, sharp rocks, knives, ninja stars, and bullets.

These riots were a daily occurrence. There was no time to identify the innocent from the guilty, and the importance of protecting one's own life was foremost in the mind of each soldier. In spite of these attacking mobs, I never witnessed any Israeli soldier wantonly shooting into a rioting crowd. We never intended to harm these Palestinian rioters, though they began the confrontations. Their use of children in this manner clearly demonstrated their devaluation of human life.

Official Israeli army policy prohibits the shooting of children being used as human shields. Israelis do not thirst for the blood of Palestinian children. Yet, children are shot, and they die because rioting is not harmless child's play. When soldiers are forced to defend themselves, innocent people get hurt. A rioting mob is not capable of rational thinking. In any part of the world, violent rioting leads to bloodshed.

One day, I watched a group of young boys playing soccer in a Gaza field. I observed them from a distance for a long time. I remember thinking that they looked like children from any part of the globe—laughing, playing, and having fun. Later, when a dozen of us went past them on a foot patrol, they ran after us, cursing and throwing rocks. Their soccer game broke up, and a few of the little boys went to inform others of our arrival. Soon after, older boys showed up and started a riot.

It saddened me to see children growing up with such virulent hatred. What kind of parent or brother or neighbor would encourage a child to participate in violent rioting? Only a parent, brother, or neighbor who places no value on human life. News reports have blasted Israel for injuring Palestinian rioters. The world should not hold Israel responsible for the practice of child martyrdom. Mr. Arafat and his regime are squarely to blame for this phenomenon. The fault lies with those who start the violence.

The United States may face this same illogical thinking because of its military actions abroad. As Robert Tracinski has astutely observed:

> . . . a sermon broadcast on Arafat-controlled television [called for murdering Jews and Americans]. . . . This is the enemy against against whom we [the United States] have urged the Israelis to exercise restraint.[3]

Terrorists do not value the lives of *their own children*, let alone those of their enemies. Israeli security forces have faced this horrific reality for years. It is difficult to preserve life while quelling a riot, but this still remains the goal of Israel's security forces. Each time I went on patrol, our commanders admonished us to use the least force possible in every situation. We regularly reviewed IDF restraint protocols, and were urged to use force only as a last resort.

It's All in Writing

A quick glance at the PLO charter (see Appendix B for selected articles) reveals that organization's valuation of terrorism as a political weapon. Article 7 states:

> . . . It is a national duty to bring up individual Palestinians in an Arab revolutionary manner. . . . He must be prepared for the armed struggle and ready to sacrifice his wealth and his life.[4]

The PA continues to impress the principles of Article 7 upon its population. During the summer of 2000, summer camps were established in Judea and Samaria. Thousands of Palestinian youths were taught to handle weapons. They carried out mock kidnappings of Israeli citizens and staged drills, where they practiced attacking Israeli military personnel. The children were taught that the execution of these activities was a national duty. The connection between such an "education" and the violent events that followed the establishment of these camps is clear.

In 1998, the Palestinian Broadcasting Authority ran a children's television program in which youngsters were taught "educational" songs such as "I Will Kill Every Jew I Meet," "Sing of My Life as a Suicide Warrior," and "When I Wander into The Entrance of Jerusalem, I Will Turn into a Suicide Warrior in Battledress."[5] The children sung these songs, all to the accolades of the show's adult host. It broke my heart to watch this despicable program. The program went against the spirit (if not the letter) of the Oslo Accords between Israel and the PA. With this typed of "education," could armed conflict between our peoples have been far away? The Palestinian Broadcasting Authority is teaching its youngsters exactly what the PLO charter of 1968 lays out. The framers of the charter sought to teach Palestinians to hate Israelis and Jews, and to prepare them for large-scale child martyrdom. Fueled by religious fervor, this phenomenon is snowballing.

Article 8 states:

> ... the phase of history in which the Palestinian people are now living is that of national struggle for the liberation of Palestine.   ... the Palestinian masses ... are one national front working for the retrieval of Palestine and its liberation through armed struggle.[6]

Here, the PLO also defines Palestinians who live in Israel, and in any nation of the world, as participants in this armed struggle. This vision of a Palestinian population actively and violently involved in a world liberation movement is a pillar of the PLO's political plans.

Article 15 adds:

> The liberation of Palestine, from an Arab viewpoint, is a national duty and it attempts to repel the Zionist and imperialist aggression against the Arab homeland, and aims at the

elimination of Zionism in Palestine. . . . Accordingly, the Arab nation must mobilize all its military, human, moral and spiritual capabilities to participate actively with the Palestinian people in the liberation of Palestine. . .[7]

This particular article sheds light on the goals of the entire charter. First, the PLO called all Arab nations and persons to use every resource at their disposal to destroy Israel. The article espouses the myth of "one Arab nation" (Pan-Arabism), working together for the same political goals. The PLO Charter calls on the Arab peoples to identify their supposed enemies, and then mobilize all resources to fight that common foe. Officially, the PA has mitigated its stance on violence against Israel by striking clauses in their charter that called for the destruction of the State of Israel.

Political Foundations

The political foundations of the *Al-Qa'eda* terrorist group can be found in the tenets of the PLO charter. The PLO drew upon the teachings of the earlier established Muslim Brotherhood organization in Egypt for much of their political inspiration. They then developed the ideology of international terror as a political weapon. The PLO/PA does not have a democratic political philosophy. In all practicality, Mr. Arafat has dictatorial powers. Democratic countries, such as the United States and Israel, change heads of state through regular elections.

Since Yassir Arafat has been the PLO/PA's strongman, Israel has elected the following prime ministers: Levi Eshkol, Golda Meir, Yitzhak Rabin (twice), Menahem Begin, Yitzhak Shamir, Shimon Peres, Binyamin Netanyahu, Ehud Barak, and Ariel Sharon. During these same years, the United States has seen the following presidents take office: Lyndon Johnson, Richard Nixon, Gerald Ford, Jimmy Carter, Ronald Reagan, George Bush, Bill Clinton, and George W. Bush. These lists demonstrate the democratic likeness between the United States and Israel. The PLO/PA's lack of executive changeover demonstrates that it has no such ideals.

In 1995, when Mr. Arafat publicly lied, saying that Israel purposefully dug into the foundations of the Mosque of Omar on Jerusalem's Temple Mount, doing so stoked the flames of both Muslim religious zeal and political discontent. Predictably, Muslim rioting on the upper Temple Mount erupted immediately. The world let

Mr. Arafat get away with crass manipulation. Why didn't the international press confront him? This falsehood caused harm to come to innocent people, both Israelis and Palestinians. Apparently, Mr. Arafat does not care about the welfare of either group.

The truth? Israel's Antiquities Authority cleared out an ancient tunnel that ran parallel to the Mosque. The activity in no way threatened its structural integrity. In fact, the rush of tourists to see the over 2,000 year old tunnel system brought business to the Muslim Quarter of Jerusalem. Mr. Arafat is aware of fundamentalist Islam's growth in PA controlled areas. Instead of attempting to mitigate its strength, he has taken advantage of extremist religious sentiment for his own political purposes. Why else did he accept and allow child martyrdom to be taught on Palestinian television? Why else did he permit summer-long terrorist training camps? Figures within the Palestinian Authority have publicly shared their sentiments regarding Israelis:

Holy War is our path. My death will be martyrdom. I will knock on the gates of Paradise with the skulls of the sons of Zion—Ayman Radi, PLO policeman and suicide bomber, 1994.[8]

We must always remember that our enemy is the Israeli occupation, and it is incumbent upon us to continue to struggle against it through the blessed intifada—Farouk Qaddumi, PLO Political Department Chair, 1994.[9]

We are going to continue the Palestinian revolution until the last martyr to create a Palestinian state—Yassir Arafat, Palestinian Authority Chairman, 30th anniversary of *Fatah*, 1995 [spoken *after* the signing of the Oslo Accords].[10]

No matter how much Mr. Arafat wishes to distance himself from Osama bin Laden, a philosophical and political connection exists between the two men. On September 24, 2001, bin Laden called on the United States to support the Palestinian cause. Whether Mr. Arafat likes it or not, bin Laden considers himself a supporter. Mr. Arafat may not wish to be allied with Osama bin laden for other political reasons, but he is not an innocent bystander in the war on terrorism. On that same day in 2001, bin Laden spoke the following words:

We hope that these brothers will be the first martyrs in the battle of Islam in this era against the new Jewish and Christian crusader campaign that is led by the Chief Crusader Bush under the banner of the cross.[11]

He was referring to the American military response to the September 11 events. His words sound eerily familiar. They are reminiscent of the rhetoric used by the PLO in past years to refer to Israel and the United States.

Chapter Six

AMERICA AND ISRAEL: ALLIES IN THE SAME WAR

Israel's Strategy Against Terror

Because of the events of September 11, Americans are now better able to understand why Israel has made preemptive strikes upon targets in Gaza, Judea, Samaria, and Lebanon. Such strikes can prevent further murders of Israelis by destroying the terror organization's infrastructure, resources, and leadership.

In spite of media portrayal of Israel as an aggressor, a preemptive strike policy has been a great help in our war against terrorism. The only alternative is to wait until Israeli citizens are murdered again, and again, and to respond to each individual situation as it occurs. Our enemies would view this strategy as a weakness. It would only encourage more attempts on Israeli lives. Preemptive strikes disrupt the plans of terror organizations, by destroying personnel and supplies. The strikes let the terrorists know that we will not sit idly by while they plot and carry out their murderous acts.

Shortly after September 11, President George W. Bush stated that American forces will hunt down the terrorists. He threatened military action against states that harbor and abate them. America's government has begun to recognize the validity of preemptive strikes as a proactive strategy in the war on terror. In his November 8, 2001 speech, President Bush noted:

> . . . in the long run, the best way to defend our homeland . . . to make sure our children live in peace is to take the battle to the enemy and stop them.[1]

This is the very idea behind Israel's policy. President Bush has validated America's right to carry out such raids. In doing so, he has also provided justification for Israel to act in like manner. President Bush noted that the United States is now targeting

"[terrorist] training camps . . . communications [infrastructures]
. . . and air defenses."[2]

Sympathy for Israel's struggle has risen since September 11. As
Tracinski noted:

> The terror we experienced [on September 11] . . . is what Is-
> raelis have lived with for decades . . . the plight of the Israelis
> was not fully real until we faced the same kind of attack here
> in America.[3]

On October 14, 2001, Israeli Prime Minister, Ariel Sharon, announced that the planned assassination of Abed Rahman Hamad
had been carried out. A *Hamas* terrorist organization mastermind,
Hamad had helped plan the June 2001 murders of twenty-three
young Israelis at a Tel Aviv discotheque. According to Israeli intelligence, Hamad was also involved in at least one other lethal terrorist
attack in Israel. If the United States can justify its bombardment of
Afghanistan as retaliation against the attacks of September 11, Israel
is justified in the obliteration of known terrorist leaders, especially
those whom Yassir Arafat and the PA refuse to arrest, jail, or extra-
dite according to the Oslo Accords.

A Common Enemy

The United States is not alone in declaring bin Laden an enemy. His
name is on Israel's "most wanted" list as well. In 1999, the Kingdom
of Jordan apprehended a number of bin Laden-trained terrorists on
their way into Israel to commit acts of terror. According to Israeli intelligence, their targets were both Israeli citizens and American tourists. It is clear that Osama bin Laden's network has targeted both of
our peoples.

In June 2000, Israeli intelligence again became aware of bin
Laden's attempts at terrorizing Israel. Nabil Ukal, a covert bin Laden
operative, was apprehended by Israeli security forces while trying to
cross into Israel from the PA territories. Ukal had been assigned to
recruit Israeli Arab citizens for a bin Laden cell. Through Ukal, bin
Laden sought to offer financial payments and terrorist training outside Israel to any Israeli Arabs who were willing to accept his offer.
Ukal was also known to have contacts within the *Hamas* terrorist
organization, and had received monetary compensation from

them.[4] Bin Laden admires *Hamas* and shares that organization's goals to eradicate Israel and the United States. There appears to be a small degree of cooperation between *Hamas* and bin Laden. *Hamas* thrives in the PA territories. According to the Institute for Anti-Terrorist Policies in Israel, Israel remains a top target on bin Laden's slate.

The entire radical Muslim fundamentalist movement despises the United States—from Mr. Arafat and his PLO/PA to bin Laden and *Al-Qa'eda*, from *Hamas* to the Islamic *Jihad*, from *Hizballah* to the PFLP, and from the Egyptian *Jihad* to the DFLP. These powerful organizations are influencing a younger generation of Muslims numbering in the millions. It is not just extremist states like Afghanistan and Iran that produce the *shahid*.

Columnist and veteran Middle East reporter Thomas Friedman succinctly analyzed how the radical movement grows. He wrote:

This is the game that produced bin Ladenism: Arab regimes fail to build a real future for their people. This triggers seething anger. Their young people who can get visas escape overseas. Those who can't turn to the mosque and Islam to protest. The regimes crush the violent Muslim protesters, but to avoid being charged with being anti-Muslim, the regimes give money and free reign to their most hardline. . . . Muslim clerics, while also redirecting their public's anger onto America through their press. Result: America ends up being hated, and Islam gets handed over to the most anti-modern forces. Have a nice day. [5]

Hating the United States and Israel

Concerning the relationship of radical fundamentalist Islam to the United States, Norman Podhoretz, editor of *Commentary Magazine*, wrote:

The point is that if Israel had never come into existence, or if it were magically to disappear, the United States would still stand as an embodiment of everything that most of these Arabs consider evil. Indeed, the hatred of Israel is in large part a surrogate for anti-Americanism. Israel is seen as the spearhead of the American drive for domination over the Middle East. The Jewish state is a translation, as it were, of America

into Hebrew—*the little enemy, the little Satan*—and to rid the
region of it would thus be tantamount to cleansing an area
belonging to Islam of the blasphemous political, social and
cultural influences emanating from a barbaric and murderous force. But the force, so to speak, is with America, of
which Israel is merely an instrument.[6]

Mr. Podhoretz has hit the proverbial nail on the head. Americans should not be so naïve as to think that if United States political
or economic support for Israel waned, the radical Muslim movement would view the United States in a more favorable light. In
2000, the United States was the single greatest donor of monetary
aid to Afghanistan ($177 million). Yet, the Taliban government re-
mained unmoved by this philanthropy. America's philosophical, political, and religious values were too opposed to those of the Taliban.
The United States is viewed as a cancer that infects all of humanity
because of her perceived lack of morals and her political philosophy.
Americans need to take note of this fact. Not only Taliban-led radicals felt this way. The sentiment exists throughout entire Muslim
fundamentalist movement. Tracinski noted:

> Their [fundamentalist Muslims] motive is a wider hatred for
> the West—for the free, secular society that allows us to flout
> Islamic law—for the industry, technology and economic
> freedom that makes us wealthy—for the military might that
> makes us invulnerable to conventional attack . . . not only
> because we support Israel, but because Israel shares and rep-
> resents our values.[7]

On October 13, 2000, Palestinian television broadcast these
words from Dr. Abu Halabiya, the aforementioned PA official:

> Allah, deal with the Jews, your enemies and the enemies of Is-
> lam. Deal with the crusaders, and America and Europe be-
> hind them.[8]

This language is meant to cast Jewish people, the United States,
and even Europe as enemies of Islam. Bin Laden himself could have
uttered these same words. In the same broadcast, Abu Halabiya called
for a *jihad* against Jews *and* the United States. By allowing these extremist broadcasts to continue, the PA condones the demonization of

the United States and Israel. The Palestinian people should not be blamed for this situation. Mr. Arafat and the PA bear responsibility for the negative attitudes. However, the Palestinian population is too often silent when their leaders threaten the very fabric of their society. The American government, and all freedom-loving societies, must call upon Yassir Arafat to crack down against this propaganda.

On June 15, 1997, Muhammad Dahlan, the former chief of Mr. Arafat's Preventative Security Service, made statements fueling a belief that the Palestinian Authority does not have any long-term interest in controlling the *Hamas* terrorist organization, despite the fact that they agreed to do so as part of the Oslo Accords. Mr. Dahlan stated:

The presence of Hamas on Palestinian territory is very important for building the Palestinian homeland.[9]

And Mr. Arafat himself remarked:

The Hamas movement is one of many patriotic movements. Even its military wing [is patriotic].[10]

The American government has officially categorized *Hamas* as a terrorist organization. The Oslo Accords bound Mr. Arafat to use his influence to curtail their activities in PA areas. Yet, consider Mr. Dahlan's words. Clearly, this has not happened.

The Palestinian press has also made revealing comments. *Al-Hayat Al-Jadida* (Arabic, The New Life) is a newspaper controlled by the PA. Editor Hafez Al-Barghouti asserted:

New York mayor Rudolph Giuliani was obsessed by his hatred of Arabs even before the terrorist attacks on New York. He hides his first name, chosen for him by his Italian father, so as not to remind the Jewish voters of the infamous Rudolph Hitler. This is why he prefers to shorten it to Rudy.[11]

Tying the name, Rudolph, to that of Adolph Hitler is quite a stretch! The article continues:

The USA is the enemy of the democratic aspirations of the Arab peoples . . . it is the number one schemer against development in the Arab world. . . . Refraining from joining the

Americans . . . is counted in the tally of the Saudi government's good deeds.[12]

The PA has been the recipient of massive amounts of American aid—aid used to help build its infrastructure. However, its propaganda organ only belittles the American government's efforts at seeking justice after the terrorist attacks perpetrated against her.

Can United States Foreign Policy Be Blamed?

Even if the United States admitted that its international policies had caused some nations to hate her, it would not make a difference. An apology would not be well received by any terrorist organization. It would not be considered a sign for rapprochement, or an initiative for a negotiated peace. It would be seen as weakness, and a lack of moral backbone. An apology would fuel even more hatred. Nothing will lessen the hostility that these terror organizations, their personnel, their financiers, and sponsoring governments have toward America. Nothing. This cannot be emphasized too strongly.

Examining American political and economic motives is a good practice for a democracy. Regular elections provide strong motivation for leaders to remain responsible. Yet, the United States must recognize that radical Muslim terrorist organizations do *not* share the same moral value system that they do. The extremists do not look inward to check their motivation, nor are they concerned if their actions cause hostility. Such concerns would be regarded as madness. These networks *want* to engender hatred of the western world and destroy society.

In reaction to the attacks on their home soil, some Americans wanted the United States to distance itself from Israel. Proponents of this attitude thought that such a move would convince militant Muslim terrorists to cease further attacks on American interests. German Foreign Minister Joschka Fischer noted how naïve this train of thought is:

> Bin Laden's aim is to create a revolution in the entire Middle East, to establish his autocratic regime, to evict the US from the region and to destroy Israel. In the Middle East conflict, Israel's existence plays an emotional role for the Arab masses. . . . But the direct causality, "Solve the Middle East

conflict [between Israel and the Palestinians] and there will
be no terrorism" is definitely fraudulent. Look at Algeria,
Iraq, Afghanistan, and Kashmir. You won't solve those conflicts by peace between the Israelis and Palestinians.[13]

*Radical Muslim terrorist organizations want to destroy the United
States, regardless of her policy toward Israel!* In 1998, when *Al-Qa'eda*-
linked terrorists bombed United States embassies in Kenya and Tanzania, some Americans asked their government to distance itself
from Israel. Former senior State Department official Abraham
Sofaer, in an interview shortly afterward, was taken aback by these
calls to dissolve America's support of Israel. Sofaer noted that some
Americans jumped to the erroneous conclusion that the relationship between the United States and Israel caused the attacks.[14] The
Irish Times quoted bin Laden on November 3, 2001.

"Those who make a distinction between America and Israel
are traitors."[15]

A change in American policy toward Israel will not have any effect on future attacks. Muslim radicals believe that the United States
is a deserving target—in and of itself, regardless of its relationship
with Israel. According to the militant Islamic point of view, both the
United States and Israel merit destruction, each one individually,
due to their positions in today's world.

The spread of anthrax in the United States caused panic and in a
few tragic cases, death. Concerned about exposure to anthrax spores,
some Americans went to Mexico to buy antibiotics. This is exactly the
type of fear and social unrest that the terrorists wish to spread. Americans may do some soul-searching, but the bin Laden network, *Hamas*,
Hizballah, the Islamic *Jihad*, the DFLP, and much of the PA, in addition to their sponsoring states, will *still* want to destroy the United
States and her interests. With these movements gaining influence,
even countries like Egypt, which has a formal peace treaty with Israel,
are unwilling to battle the voices of hatred within their societies. As
Italian journalist Fiamma Nirenstein observed:

Wherever one looks, from Cairo and Gaza to Damascus and
Baghdad, from political and religious figures to writers and
educators, from lawyers to pop stars, and in every organ of
the media, the very people with whom the state of Israel is

expected to live in peace have devoted themselves with ever greater ingenuity to slandering and demonizing the Jewish state.[16]

Among other things, Nirenstein was probably referring to the disturbing 2001 number one hit song in Egypt entitled "I Hate Israel." She accurately described the tragic situation in the Middle East.

Anthony Cordesman, a senior fellow at the Center for Strategic and International Studies of Georgetown University, noted that four things are necessary to defeat international terrorism: solid leadership, persistence, focus, and decisiveness. This was defined as using force against specific organizations, developing strategies particular to each group, developing the military, economic, diplomatic, and information wings of a defense system, and a willingness to do battle over a long period of time.[17]

Mr. Cordesman's advice is wise. He advocates the types of proactive measures that Israel has been taking for over half a century. Yet, on most occasions, international response to our strikes on terrorist training camps, supply depots, terror organization leaders and their headquarters has been overwhelmingly negative.

Again, many Americans may now have a new appreciation of Israel's preemptive strategy. If, by engaging in similar efforts, the United States might have avoided the events of September 11, surely the Western world would have done everything possible. Israel has had no choice but to go after the terrorists out to destroy her. As an American Marine officer wrote:

> [I] recognize the inherent differences between Israeli and U.S. political realities. Israel, surrounded by hostile borders, must take extraordinary precautions to protect itself. The U.S. does not find itself in the same geo-political spectrum as Israel. What may be an unacceptable response in a certain situation can, and does, become not only acceptable, but morally right under other circumstances.[18]

Mr. Cordesman noted that the United States must now "strike at windows of opportunity . . . [and] . . . be decisive, hunt them [the terrorists] down and kill them, as silently as possible." He was also astute enough to realize that "half measures won't work." This strategy will not change the aims, ends, financing, or recruiting policies of international Arab terrorist organizations, but it will, to some extent, curtail their plans for a short period of time.[19]

President Bush emphasized this reality on September 20, 2001:

... it [the war on terrorism] will not end until every terrorist group in global reach has been found, stopped and defeated. ... America should not expect one battle but a lengthy campaign, unlike any other we have seen.[20]

Although this is a relatively new realization for Americans, Israelis have understood these issues for a long time. Israel has been a leader in the battle against these same organizations, which, as President Bush observed, "follow in the path of fascism and Nazism."[21] Both countries are engaged in a lengthy campaign against a common enemy. Israel and the United States can help one another. Much empathy already exists between our two nations. America has supported Israel since our inception in 1948. Yet, the 1990s saw a decline in popular sympathy for Israel's plight, when the PLO attempted, mainly through the media, to convince the world that Israel had been the aggressor in its relations with Palestinians, and therefore unfaithful to her Oslo Accord commitments.

Can the United States Afford to Leave Israel Out of the Picture?

In spite of Israel being the natural ally of the United States in the current war on terror, some voices of American government call for leaving Israel out of the picture in order to play to Muslim sensitivities. Israel's participation in an American-led campaign against terrorism would be viewed by even "moderate" Arab and Muslim governments as enough of a reason to preclude their involvement. Fortunately, many leaders understand the intrinsic connection between Israel and the United States in the war against terror. Senator Mitch McConnell, the current ranking minority member of the Senate Foreign Operations Subcommittee, called upon both countries to work together:

America cannot win the war against terrorism without Israel. Israel has the experience, dedication and freedom that are absolutely necessary to prevail over these fanatics. We must stand arm-in-arm with our ally.[22]

Agreeing with Senator McConnell, Chicago columnist Joseph Aaron wrote:

America needs to cling tight to those who will truly be with us. In the end, in essence, it will be the job of the United States, the UK and the State of Israel to win this war [against terrorism]. For in the end, most will say this is America's problem, just as it was said "this is the Jews' problem" after Kristallnacht. . . . As long as they were just blowing up Israeli kids waiting to get into a disco and pregnant Jewish women having lunch in a Jerusalem pizzeria, terrorism was the Jews' problem. September 11, 2001 showed us that the Jews' problem is now the world's.[23]

German Foreign Minister Joschka Fischer stated:

It would be a major mistake to try to isolate Israel. . . . it is important that we [the Alliance] make clear . . . that Israel is not alone, and will never be alone. . . . in times like these, this should be especially emphasized.[24]

Truly, America and Israel are allies in the same war.

Chapter Seven

RELATIONSHIPS WITH MUSLIM NATIONS

Creating a Coalition

The American government seems set to create a wide coalition to help fight bin Laden and his *Al-Qa'eda* organization, as well as other terrorist groups around the globe. This is a reasonable strategy. However, the United States is attempting to enlist a number of Muslim countries to join in the battle. Hence, the United States is allying itself with some of Israel's declared enemies.

Noted American journalist, William Safire, argued for getting as many Muslim countries as possible involved in the coalition against bin Laden, *Al-Qa'eda*, and other Muslim terrorist organizations. He recommended that a Muslim foreign legion be formed.[1] Mr. Safire fails to recognize a crucial aspect of the collective Muslim psyche. It is highly doubtful that such a Muslim force could ever involve itself in a Western led coalition against other Muslim countries or organizations. It is well known that the Gulf War alliance, led by the United States, included a number of Muslim governments. The United States had to be very careful not to do anything to offend Muslim members of the Gulf War alliance, at the risk of their pulling out.

In his aforementioned article, Mr. Safire admits that there is a "real reluctance of well-known Muslim clergy who are willing to preach more than "don't blame Muslims [for the acts of September 11]."[2] There is no united or authoritative Islamic clerical condemnation of radical Muslim terror. Why is this the case? Why do we not hear Muslim clergy around the globe issuing a condemnation of what occurred on September 11, 2001? Why hasn't the United States' closest Arab ally, Egypt, taken a more active role in the emerging coalition?

I gained insight into some of these issues when I was a university student in the United States. A Muslim Moroccan classmate, who was not particularly religious, hoped to stay in America, obtain citizenship, and find his piece of the "American dream". We studied together and got along well; we were more than just acquaintances. It never seemed to bother him that I was an Israeli, nor did it hinder him from speaking with me.

One day as we were walking together, he made the following statement. "I accept you as a Jew. No problem. This is America, and all ethnic groups are here. I am a Muslim but I don't pray, and I don't attend any mosque. I don't want to, either. I am liberal. I date Christian girls and I go out at night to have fun. But if you ever insult Islam in any way, shape or form, I will attack you physically." I was surprised by has nasty demeanor. I had never said anything about his religious beliefs. We were not talking about religion or politics. I didn't understand why he had brought up this subject at this time. This otherwise gentle, mild-mannered student was unwilling to condone any action he thought would betray or insult his religion, although he didn't practice it. The thought of a non-Muslim berating Islam gave him the right to lash out at me.

Of course, one cannot generalize and say that this is the way of all Muslims. Yet the Israeli daily *Ma'ariv* (Hebrew, Evening News) reported that a in survey among British Muslims, forty percent of those polled felt it would be right for them to join the Taliban in Afghanistan to wage war against the Alliance. Ninety-six percent responded that the United States needed to immediately stop its air assaults against the Taliban. Seventy-three percent felt that British Prime Minister Tony Blair erred in supporting American-led initiatives against the Taliban, and sixty-one percent stated that efforts to capture bin Laden were unjustified. In fact, there were calls within the British Muslim community to send youngsters to Afghanistan to support the Taliban.[3]

Those who took part in this survey represented a diverse and somewhat Westernized population. Thus, the survey indicates that there is a strong reluctance among Muslims to oppose one another in the political arena.

Saudi Arabia

Americans may be unnerved to learn that Saudi Arabia, while maintaining her stance as an ally of the United States, has continued to finance international terrorist organizations. Most Western observers consider Saudi Arabia to be a moderate Arab state. Many Israelis do not agree with this assessment.

The Saudis have actively participated in military conflicts against Israel, in the War of Independence, and again in the 1967 and 1973 wars. It is not in America's best interests to overlook the fact that Saudi Arabia has financed enemies of the United States. However, this truth has been overlooked because of the importance of maintaining friendly relations with Saudi Arabia. Mayor Rudolph Giuliani is to be applauded for refusing a ten million-dollar relief donation from Saudi prince Alwalid bin Talal. The prince stated:

At times like this one, we must address some of the issues that led to such a criminal attack. The government of the United States should re-examine its policies in the Middle East and adopt a more balanced stance toward the Palestinian cause . . . our Palestinian brethren continue to be slaughtered at the hands of Israelis while the world turns the other cheek.[4]

Mayor Giuliani rebuffed him:

There is no moral equivalent to this attack. . . . Not only are those statements [by Prince Alwalid] wrong, they are part of the problem.[5]

Mayor Giuliani was outraged at the prince's attempts to justify the September 11 murders. Prince Alwalid's criticism of American and Israeli policy, could have been echoed by bin Laden. Blaming American policy toward Israel for the September 11 attacks is wrong. It overlooks the fact that bin Laden and his murderous network would want to destroy the United States *even if Israel did not exist.* The Saudi government has done very little to help solve the crisis between Israel and the Palestinians.

So far, Saudi Arabia has refused to allow the United States to use their military bases for air strike launches in Operation Enduring Freedom. Why? The Saudi family believes they are the true guardians of worldwide Islam. Therefore, they cannot and will not be a party to an attack on another Muslim nation or group. One might argue that the Saudis allowed American military operations to be launched from their soil during the Gulf War. However, this was because the maniacal Saddam Hussein had threatened to destroy Saudi Arabia. Turning to the United States-led alliance for help and protection was their only option. The Saudis knew that their military could not have stopped a sustained Iraqi assault, had it occurred.

United States assistance was strategic in rescuing Saudi Arabia and Kuwait out of their dire straits. Yet, ten years later, the religious sensibilities of these two nations prevent them from allying themselves with other Muslim nations against bin Laden. This is the sad reality of the situation. According to the Muslim worldview, all of mankind is divided into two "houses," believing Muslims and unbelievers. Because of this doctrine, even moderate Muslim heads of state will not take action against the "house of believers," even if represented by men such as Osama bin Laden. As of today, Turkey has been the sole exception to this policy. Saudi Arabia does not appear concerned with stopping *Al-Qa'eda* unless it threatens their government's existence. The colloquial phrase, "see no evil, hear no evil," accurately assesses Saudi awareness of radical Muslim terrorist activity.

Recent statements from the Saudi press should be disturbing to Americans. The Saudi newspaper, *Al-Riyadh*, ran an anti-Semitic clolumn, worthy of an American slander lawsuit. The article, "Al-Walid's Check, The Homosexual Governor [George Pataki of New York] and the Propaganda War" cited the prince's rejected donation to New York City:

> The words of [Prince Alwalid] did not . . . please the Jewish lobby in the home of the largest Jewish community in the world [New York]. Because the governor of the Big Apple is Jewish, he refused to [accept the prince's monetary donation] and caused a storm. . . . Giuliani said, "What we [America] must do is kill 6,000 innocent people [in retribution]." . . .The problem is with Giuliani, not with the declarations of Prince Alwalid. . . . Giuliani denied the victims of the building that collapsed the aid they need. He sacrificed the public interest for a private interest, manifested in his desire to draw closer to the Jewish electorate.[6]

From time to time, Saudi Arabia, a "moderate state," formally calls for a *jihad* against Israel. By doing so, the Saudis demonstrate their desire to further the stereotype of Israelis as the eternal enemy of all Muslims. This is *not* a "moderate" attitude. It may be that the Saudis issue their calls simply to underscore their belief that they are the protectors of the Muslim world. As the state possessing control over the holy sites of Mecca and Medina, the Saudi government has always seen itself as the guardian of the faith. Furthermore, the official state religion of Saudi Arabia is *Wahhabi* (Arabic, followers of Abd-Al-Wahhab, the movement's founder) Islam. Being members of this sect has added to their protector-guardian complex. The Saudis believe that their sect practices the purest form of Islam. Saudi financing of terrorist activities against Israel is akin to participating in a *jihad*.

The Saudi government continues to portray itself as a friend of the United States. On December 10, 2001, the *Boston Globe* carried a full-page advertisement from the Saudi government reading, "Two nations. One goal."[7] Adorning the page was a dove, along with the Saudi flag next to the American flag. The implied message was that the Saudi and American nations share the same objectives. If this is true, why did the Saudis refuse to respond to the United States' plea to cut off funding to *Al-Qa'eda* and other Muslim terrorist organizations immediately after September 11? If the United States and Saudi Arabia have similar ideologies, why hasn't Saudi Arabia extradited the brutal former Ugandan dictator Idi Amin, forcing him to face justice? Instead, Amin has found safe harbor in Saudi Arabia. Protecting murderous dictators is not consistent with American ideals.

A close examination of the *Boston Globe* ad reveals the words on the Saudi flag, "There is no God but Allah, and Muhammad is His prophet." This is not the creed upon which the United States was founded, nor does it represent the American ideals of life, liberty, and the pursuit of happiness. If American and Saudi national goals are similar, why are United States citizens working in Saudi Arabia forced to live a shut-in existence, with no freedom to share their religious convictions? Why are they not permitted to travel about freely as they do at home, or as Saudi citizens do in the United States? The civil rights that are cherished in the United States do not exist in Saudi Arabia. Perhaps the Boston Globe ad was the Saudi government's way of attempting to quell the criticism it received in response to Prince Alwalid's statements during his run-in with Mayor Giuliani.

A Saudi presence in an American-led alliance might be seen as merely cosmetic. Most Muslims nations cannot support the United States in its military actions against other Islamic countries. Therefore, if the protector of Islam, Saudi Arabia, is willing to join an American-led coalition, all Muslim countries should do the same.

Saudi Arabia might join such an alliance in word—but not in deed, and only in order to stay on the good side of the United States and Western Europe. Her participation would only be a pretense. There would be little, if any, practical involvement.

Perhaps due to American pressure for accountability, the Saudi government recently showed small signs of moderating their stand. In February 2002, the newspaper, *A-Sharq Al-Awsat* (Arabic, The Middle East) denounced the manner in which Yassir Arafat handled the *Karine A* weapons shipment ordeal. Loaded with fifty tons of military hardware, the vessel was in transit between Iran and the PA territories. Initially, the Saudi press supported Mr. Arafat's assertion that he knew nothing of the event. Later, Arafat admitted that as leader of the PA, it was his responsibility to know about these things. Ahmad Al-Rab'i, a reporter for *A-Sharq Al-Awsat*, censured Mr. Arafat, calling him deceptive and accusing him of misleading the Saudi public.[8] This was one small step in the right direction.

Yet, the March 2002 Saudi overture of peace toward Israel was puzzling. The Saudi royal government stated:

Arab nations stress their intention to realize a lasting and comprehensive peace but at the same time Israel must show its good faith toward peace.[9]

What would the Saudi government call Israel's signing of the Oslo Accords? Were not our donations of weapons and money to the PA to build their state a sign of good faith? Former Prime Minister Ehud Barak was willing to give up the Golan Heights and part of the city of Jerusalem. Somehow, the Saudi government fails to realize *how much* goodwill Israel has already demonstrated in an attempt to forge peace with the Arab world. Saudi Arabia called on Israel to unilaterally withdraw from all of Judea, Samaria, and Gaza, and grant the legitimate rights of the Palestinians, including the creation of an independent state with Jerusalem as its capital. The Saudis stated that such Israelis overtures would be met with "complete peace" from Arab nations.

Given the fact that a minority of Arab nations agreed to participate in the Saudi initiative, positive results seem doubtful. Since Mr. Barak offered the same concessions that are called for in the Saudi proposal, what is the difference between the two offers? Due to the Palestinian Authority's intransigence, there was never any serious movement toward the acceptance of Mr. Barak's concessions. Therefore, on what basis should Israelis now believe these "new" Saudi promises?

I would be more convinced of Saudi Arabia's desire for peace in the Middle East if articles like the following never made it to press. A article written on the Jewish holiday of Purim, by Dr. Umayma Ahmad Al-Jalamah and published in the Saudi daily *Al-Riyadh* on March 10, 2002, read:

Unfortunately, this filling [for Purim pastries] cannot be left out, or substituted with any alternative serving the same purpose. For this holiday, the Jewish people must obtain human blood so that their clerics can prepare the pastries. In other words, the practice cannot be carried out as required if human blood is not spilled! Before I go into the details, I would like to clarify that the Jews spilling human blood to prepare pastry for their holidays is a well-established fact, historically and legally, all throughout history. This was one of the main reasons for the persecution and exile that were their lot in Europe and Asia at various times. Let us now examine how the victims' blood is spilled. For this, a needle-studded barrel is used; this is a kind of barrel, about the size of the human body, with extremely sharp needles set in it on all sides. [These needles] pierce the victim's body, from the moment he is placed in the barrel. These needles do the job, and the victim's blood drips from him very slowly. Thus, the victim suffers dreadful torment—torment that affords the Jewish vampires great delight as they carefully monitor every detail of the blood-shedding with pleasure and love that are difficult to comprehend. After this barbaric display, the Jews take the spilled blood, in the bottle set in the bottom [of the needle-studded barrel], and the Jewish cleric makes his coreligionists completely happy on their holiday when he serves them the pastries in which human blood is mixed. There is another way to spill the blood: The victim can be slaughtered as a sheep is slaughtered, and his blood collected in a container. Or, the victim's veins can be slit in several places, letting his blood drain from his body. This blood is very carefully collected—as I have already noted—by the rabbi, the Jewish cleric, the chef who specializes in preparing these kinds of pastries. The human race refuses even to look at the Jewish pastries, let alone prepare them or consume them![10]

Dr. Al-Jalamah's lies reveal his intent to defame both Israel and the Jewish people. This type of questionable journalism is nothing short of media-sponsored warfare against Israel. It consists of the historic blood libel accusation, which has repeatedly been proven to be untrue and based solely on anti-Semitic motivations. Veteran Middle Eastern news reporter David Dolan recently commented:

> The fact that many people living within the borders of the United States' closest Arab allies hold such strong anti-American views is not primarily due to Washington's support for Israel, or our robust democratic values and economic prosperity. It is part and parcel of the general Islamic worldview that Muslims should, and one day will, rule the world, not America or other Western infidel countries. Post 9/11 negative American impressions of Arabs in general will not be helped by the Gallup findings that 61% of all Muslims surveyed do not believe that Arabs carried out the New York and Washington attacks. An astounding 89% of Kuwaitis think that any but Arab terrorists did the dirty deed, which is probably about what the findings would have been *in neighboring Saudi Arabia* if the autocratic government there had allowed that sensitive question to be asked.[11] (*italics mine*)

Dolan's comments provide insight into how the United States is perceived in supposed moderate countries, such as Kuwait and Saudi Arabia. Robert McFarlane, one of former President Ronald Reagan's national security advisers, suggested that the United States should pressure Saudi Arabia and the Gulf States into censuring all militant Muslim terror. He also advised the United States to pressure European governments to put an end to harboring convicted terrorists. McFarlane asserted that European governments must go all out in arresting and extraditing them.[12]

On September 19, 2001, L. Paul Bremer, former United States Ambassador-at-Large for Counter-Terrorism, made public that which Israel has claimed and tried to convince the Western of world for a long time: Syria aids and finances international terror. He stated that Syria houses fourteen terrorist training camps and suggested that the United States pressure European businesses to stop doing business with states that sponsor terror organizations.[13] It would serve the United States well to insist that the Saudis end any encouragement of Syrian-sponsored state terrorism.

Egypt

Egypt's President Mubarak claims he wants to maintain peace with Israel, although he makes no effort toward helping his people think positively of Israelis. He has not helped to stop slander against Israel in the Egyptian media. Peace with Israel brings Egypt more benefits than war. Egypt's alliance with the United States provides much needed economic and military assistance. A war with Israel would threaten this ongoing support.

Mr. Mubarak finds himself in an uncomfortable position, politically and religiously. A large Muslim fundamentalist movement is alive and growing in Egypt. If this movement gained political power, Egypt's peace treaty with Israel would be threatened as well as its relationship with the United States. Although Mr. Mubarak would like to see bin Laden and *Al-Qa'eda* destroyed, because they represent a threat to his government, he cannot take action. He would be risking his political life.

The Egyptian press, possibly representing rising popular sentiments, has lashed out against United States-led initiatives in Afghanistan, blaming Israel for many aspects of the conflict. The Egyptian government controls much of the press. It has adopted a contradictory stance vis-à-vis American-led initiatives against terrorism. *Al-Ahram* (Arabic, The Pyramids), Egypt's semi-official government newspaper, noted:

Egypt stated that terror should be struck with full force . . . [At the same time] Egypt emphasized that efforts to strike at terrorism must not lead to damage to innocent civilians. . . . Egypt maintained that the American war against terrorism need not lead to attacks on any Arab or Islamic countries, which will, if it happens, constitute cruel and stupid aggression that will . . . serve Israel's interests.[14]

Al-Ahram continued:

American missiles and bombs have nothing to hit in Afghanistan. Instead of cutting this stage short, the American forces have greatly expanded it. . . . there were several reports that the humanitarian materials [airdropped by Alliance forces to Afghanis] have been genetically treated, with the aim of affecting the health of the Afghani people.[15]

Egypt's semi-official newspaper is stating that Mubarak's government backs an American war against terrorism that takes no military initiatives! This statement by *Al-Ahram* is contradictory and misleading. Should the United States conduct its war on terrorism solely through diplomatic means? President Bush attempted to do this on the days following September 11. He tried to reason with the Taliban government, but they refused to cooperate.

Additionally, the charge of genetically altering humanitarian food supplies was meant to cast a negative light on American efforts in Afghanistan. *Al-Ahram* told its readers that America was poisoning Afghanis! President Mubarak has not criticized his media's censure of American actions. His silence is not the result of a desire to uphold the freedom of the press. He remains quiet so as not to offend the fundamentalist sector of his population. Mr. Mubarak is taking a *laissez-faire* approach to confronting radical Islamic fervor.

The Egyptian government newspaper *Al-Akbar* (Arabic, The News) has charged the American press with waging a terrorist campaign against Egypt. It stated:

> The campaign of hatred and incitement against Egypt currently being waged by the *Washington Post* and The *New York Times* is a good example of the new terrorists whose voice is rising in the West.[16]

Sympathies with bin Laden's political extremism and fundamentalist religious beliefs run high among the Egyptian population. Any overt action Mubarak might take against bin Laden would rile this sector of society, and could threaten Mubarak's political life and Egypt's social order. On October 9, 2001, some twenty thousand students at Cairo University protested American-led military strikes against *Al-Qa'eda* and Taliban sites. Veteran Middle East scholar Walter Laqueur commented, "Some Muslim governments abhor terrorists, no doubt, but they fear public opinion even more."[17] The Egyptian president does not appreciate the rising tide of Muslim fundamentalism within his country, but he will take no action against it unless it threatens his very existence.

This reality has doomed President Bush's attempts to involve Mubarak in an anti-bin Laden coalition. Mr. Mubarak *can* serve as an advisor to such a coalition, and offer tacit support. He has ordered crackdowns against violence when foreign tourists have been murdered in his country. However, he is quite reticent to ask Egyptian Muslim clerics to censure the violence of September 11. President Mubarak's his hands are tied. He needs to continue to find ways to maintain a cold peace with Israel while only verbally supporting the American-led military initiative against terrorism.

Thus, Egypt, the Arab country to which America gives the most financial and military aid, cannot give America much in return during her hour of need. A growing number of Egyptians do not appreciate this American aid, which is seen as an attempt by an infidel power to interfere with Egypt's internal affairs.

Peace between Israel and Egypt continues to exist, in spite of the fact that Egypt has not fulfilled tourism and trade promises, and in spite of inflammatory remarks in the Arab press. Statements, such as this one from *Al-Ahram*, abound:

It would not be an exaggeration to say that the heroic and *fidaai* (Arabic, martyrdom) warriors are the only light in the dark skies, they are the sole remaining sign of life in the Arab nation. . . . If we can still lift our heads with pride, it is only because we still have as models those young men who chose to die so that our lives would have hope and meaning and so that our long night will see a dawn with a message of hope.[18]

Another *Al-Ahram* article stated:

For many long years, America made many peoples in the world cry. It was always America that carried out the acts; now, acts are being carried out against it. A cook who concocts poison must one day also taste that poison.[19]

A columnist from the Egyptian newspaper *Al-Maydan* (Arabic, The Field) noted:

Millions across the world shouted in joy [about September 11]. America was hit! This call expressed the sentiments of millions across the world, whom the American master had treated with tyranny, arrogance, bullying, conceit, deceit and bad taste—like every bully whom no one has yet put in his place.[20]

Writing for the Arab daily, *Al-Usbu' Al-Adabi* (Arabic, [Syrian] Writer's Association), another reporter observed:

> Bush was woken from . . . his dream of false power by this blow [the events of September 11], from which, I think, he will never recover. Bush, drink from the bitter cup of the blood of your people, so that you will know that Allah is just![21]

Given the nature of what is happening in Egyptian society today, I am not optimistic about the true normalization of relations between Israel and Egypt. As long as President Mubarak is in power, Egypt will probably continue on an unsteady course, attempting to balance relationships with the United States and the larger Muslim world.

Jordan

King Abdallah of Jordan maintains an official peace with Israel. His desire to do so is quite practical. As King Hussein, his father, struggled to do, Abdallah attempts to maintain his stability as a minority ruler. Jordan has its own growing Muslim fundamentalist movement, and although it is not as large or as strong as its Egyptian counterpart, it represents a threat to the ruling Hashemite family, to which King Abdallah belongs. Jordan cannot afford any conflicts with Israel. Border problems could result in a popular uprising against Abdallah. He will survive best in an atmosphere of peace.

Egypt and Jordan are the only two neighboring countries with which Israel holds working peace treaties. With the signed Oslo Accords dead in the water, Israel is again adrift in a sea of Arab unwillingness to extend her equality as a Middle Eastern nation. Given current religious and political sensitivities, there is little hope that this situation will ever improve, short of the Messiah coming and changing the world order.

Syrian Sponsorship of Hizballah

The *Hizballah* terrorist organization has infiltrated a number of Middle Eastern countries including Syria.

The AIPAC organization, an American pro-Israel congressional lobby group wrote:

Hezbollah's ability to wreak havoc on the international community is primarily due to its state sponsorship by Iran and Syria. . . . Successive Syrian governments have encouraged Hezbollah to launch attacks against Israel from southern Lebanon.[22]

Hizballah has murdered American Marines serving in Lebanon. They are implicated in the slaying of American soldiers stationed in Saudi Arabia and have killed some 276 United States soldiers worldwide. They have also been credited with the butchering of 100 Argentineans, 58 French soldiers, and scores of Israelis. The hijacking of TWA flight 847 in 1985 is also their handiwork.

Syria's sponsorship of *Hizballah* should cause great international concern. The United States would do well to give strong ultimatums to Syria regarding its involvement in terrorist activities. In light of inflammatory remarks in the Syrian press regarding the September 11 attacks, the United States may want to reevaluate its overall relationship with that nation. Here are two examples of such comments:

The American government had contaminated my humanity, and I began to say to myself, when I saw the masses fleeing in horror in the streets of New York and Washington, "Let them drink of the cup that their government has given all the peoples to drink from: first and foremost, our people."[23]

And:

I felt deep within me like someone that was delivered from the grave. I felt that I was being carried in the air above the corpse of the mythological symbol of arrogant American imperialist power. . . . My lungs filled with air and I breathed in relief, as I had never breathed before.[24]

Pakistan

The atmosphere in Pakistan is fragile. The government has thrown in its lot with the American-led alliance against bin Laden and *Al-*

Qa'eda. Due to the Pakistani government's stand, a radical fundamentalist backlash is a developing. Pakistan's small Christian community fears severe persecution by Muslim extremists because of the American-led attacks against Afghanistan.

Pakistani Christians have expressed concern about the risk of mass genocide. Many believe that Islamic radicals have all but paralyzed the country with daily violent riots and terrorist activity. On October 28, 2001, in Behalwalpur, sixteen Pakistani Christians were murdered during an attack on a church. Such heinous acts of intolerance may increase because political mechanisms are in place that sometimes make it easy for extremists to get away with their crimes. As able as Pakistan's government may be in controlling outward violence and rioting, it cannot control the fomenting religious fervor within its borders.

Because of assisting the United States and Britain by lending ground space for military bases, Pakistan's government may need to defend itself against an increasingly hostile population within its borders. On October 27, 2001, Associated Press correspondent Riaz Khan reported that some five thousand Pakistanis left for Afghanistan to help defend the Taliban. He noted:

> Thousands of Pakistani men, young and old, had massed in Temergarah on Friday night with assault rifles, machine guns and rocket launchers. A few even carried axes and swords. Their mission, they said, was to enter Afghanistan's Kunar province and help that country's ruling Taliban defend against any ground incursions by American troops ... volunteers gathered in scores ... sitting on the ground to be briefed on the ways of "jihad"–an Islamic holy war.[25]

A television newscast reported on widespread parades of cheering crowds showing support for bin Laden and Al–Qa'eda in Northeast Pakistan on that same day.

President Pervez Musharaf asked Alliance forces to stop the bombings during Ramadan, (the holy month of fasting for Muslims), but his request was denied. President Musharaf knew that the continuation of military initiatives would inflame Pakistani Muslim passion against the coalition and his own government. Warring with the Taliban during Ramadan was seen as an immoral act against Muslims. Yet, if it was truly a moral outrage for Al–Qa'eda and the

Taliban to be attacked during Ramadan, why was there such little concern for morality when twenty Israelis were butchered by Muslim extremists during a March 27, 2002 Passover dinner? Imagine the negative reaction if Muslims were to be killed by non-Muslims as they marched in Mecca during a Ramadan observance. When it comes to applying moral standards to the Arab-Israeli conflict, the proverbial shoe does not fit on the other foot. Note that there was little, if any, outrage in the Middle East over the 1973 attack on Israel on Yom Kippur.

During Operation Enduring Freedom, American Secretary of Defense, Donald Rumsfeld, made it clear that the United States would not stop military initiatives because of Ramadan. This decision was best in terms of military tactics. By the end of the holiday, the Taliban government had fallen and *Al-Qa'eda's* infrastructure was severely damaged. As the winter of 2001–2002 approached, Alliance military objectives needed to be achieved with dispatch. Mr. Musharaf recognizes that he sits on top of a powder keg of emotions that could explode into extreme social unrest around the entire Muslim world, particularly in his country.

Other Places in the Muslim World

Libya, Iraq, Iran, the Sudan, and Lebanon will have nothing to do with any American-led coalition against terror, and may take measures to oppose it. Other Muslim nations consider themselves to be so far removed from American interests that they would never offer assistance, nor would the United States court their participation. Morocco, Tunisia, Algeria, and Yemen fall into this category.

Turkey is one nation that has taken part in Operation Enduring Freedom. Though the Turks are Muslims, they are a fiercely independent people and not an Arab nation. For many years, they have cooperated with the United States, allowing their land to be used for military bases. Israel was also granted the use of Turkish air space for Air Force training. The relationship between Turkey and Syria is problematic. Turkey is threatened by militant Muslim terrorist organizations in Syria, which consider her alliance with the United States and Israel to be traitorous to Islam.

On November 2, 2002, *The New York Times* reported that Turkey had planned to deploy special forces to Afghanistan to help battle the Taliban. Although only a small number of soldiers were actually sent, it was a symbolic gesture and demonstrated the stand of the Turkish government.[26]

The Islamic world is undergoing a transformation. Currently, 19.2% of the earth's population is Muslim. Some experts predict that by 2025, Muslims may become the most populous people group on the planet due to their high birthrate. Therefore, Islamic radicalization presents a challenge for Western society. A socio-political war is being waged against the free world. The question of who will wield greatest political clout in the future is at the heart of this conflict.

Mixing Politics and Religion

Muslim terrorists have mixed radical Fundamentalist Islam with modern nationalism. The result of this incendiary combination is the fomenting of a violent movement, which desires to mold the world according to its wishes. It is difficult to make a distinction between religious and political motivations; more often than not, they merge.

One cannot minimize the influence of widespread anger in today's Muslim world. This animosity is directed toward affluent Western states, who are perceived as accumulating their wealth through the oppression of Islamic nations and people. Some of the anger is also vented at Muslim governments, such as those of Saudi Arabia, Oman, Abu Dhabi, and Bahrain, which have become wealthy through oil sales to the Western world. This combination of fundamentalist Islam and radical politics has created the atmosphere conducive to acts of cruelty against Israel and more recently, the United States. Binyamin Netanyahu stated:

> The durability of the twin fanaticisms of Pan-Arab nationalism and Islamic fundamentalism—their militarism, xenophobia, irredentism and irreducible hatred of the existing order—is the true core of conflict in the Middle East, and of much of the violence that emanates from that region to the rest of the world.[27]

Mr. Netanyahu has fingered the true causes behind what happened to America on September 11, as well as what has been happening to Israel for so many years. Combine Arab nationalism with radical Muslim fundamentalism, and too often, the result has been terrorism.

Chapter Eight

COPING WITH TERRORISM

How does one live life in view of present terrorist threats? How does one cope in the aftermath of a terrorist incident? How do we gain our lives back and teach our children not to be in constant fear? How do we build lives for ourselves when at any moment they can be snatched away? How do I, as an Israeli and a Jew, teach my children not to hate all Arabs and Muslims?

All victims of militant Islamic terror have had to struggle with these or similar questions. These issues are practical and not merely theoretical. In days ahead, many Americans will be consumed with finding answers. Nazi concentration camp survivor and Nobel prize-winning author Elie Weisel wrote:

> Faced with such immense suffering, how can one go on working, studying and simply living without sinking into despair? How is one to vanquish the fear that infiltrated our very existence? And how are we to console the families and friends of the more than 5000 victims.[1]

When terrorism rears its ugly head, one is in shock. The more serious the terrorist attack, the greater the mental and physical trauma for its victims. After each attack in which I was involved, I went into a type of shock. My ability to think and rationalize was impaired. Emotionally, I felt numb. After the shock wore off, I had a strong desire for revenge, while feeling immense gratitude for still being alive.

After a while, the numbness, heightened emotions, and want for revenge began to pass. The sympathy, prayers, and good wishes of family and friends, including my doctor and a few government officials, helped to alleviate the pain. My appreciation of the emotional anguish that Holocaust survivors experienced grew immensely. Although I would not, of course, equate my experience with theirs.

The Jewish *hagomel* prayer (words of thanksgiving when one has lived through a life-threatening situation) is appropriate for times like these. It leads one to focus on the mercy of the Holy One of Israel, instead of concentrating on feelings of anger. Trying to make sense of the contrasting emotions is not easy. When terrorist attacks ended in death, I grieved. Sadness and anger welled up in me. Often, I experienced a sense of lethargy, unable to go about my daily business. I mourned and mourned—sometimes for days, sometimes for a month, often longer. Having a supportive network was helpful. Being able to talk about what was going on inside of me was also important. Believing in a God to whom I could pray, a God in whom I could rely—even if I did not have all the answers, made all the difference.

In Israel, terrorism is a constant topic of discussion. These types of conversations are healthy. I recommend that terrorist victims surround themselves with caring friends, find some type of private counseling, and take advantage of a victim's support group. Books on the subject are also helpful. In *Trauma and Recovery*, Dr. Judith Herman recounts stories of American Vietnam War veterans. She analyzes the effects of the traumas they suffered and recommends methods of treatment.

Terror traumatizes not only individuals, but also a nation's collective memory. The horrific events of September 11, 2001 and the December 7, 1941 attack on Pearl Harbor will be engraved upon hearts of Americans forever. The attack on Pearl harbor forced the United States into World War II, and became the watchword for victory over the regimes of Hirohito, Hitler, and Mussolini. Similarly, Americans will recall the attacks of September 11, 2001 as the trigger that set off their nation's active participation in the war against terrorism.

Every time a terrorist attack has struck Israel, I have asked the unanswerable question, "Why?" In the aftermath of September 11, we all ponder the same enigma. Once again, Elie Weisel, someone who saw the depths of human depravity, offers profound words:

> Can it [terror] be explained? Yes, by hatred. Hatred is the root of evil everywhere. . . . In its name, all seems permitted. For those who glorify hatred, as terrorists do, the end justifies all means, including the most despicable ones.[2]

In the mid-1990s, on the day after a Jordania soldier viciously attacked and murdered a group of Israeli schoolgirls, the newspapers showed photos of the youngsters. I did not know them or their families. Yet, I grieved over the loss of these innocent children.

Israel mourns each fatality. Every year, in a national experience of indescribable emotions, our country embraces the grief of Holocaust survivors and their families on Holocaust and Heroes' Remembrance Day. We remember them through the personal stories of elderly survivors, which are broadcast on radio and television. And, as is so common in Jewish life, we try to glean whatever moral lessons we can from the suffering. On this day, we also honor the Righteous Gentiles, those non-Jews in Europe who hid Jewish families and resisted Nazi terrorism.

A week after Holocaust and Heroes' Remembrance Day, Israel holds Memorial Day, a time to mourn Israel's fallen soldiers. Family and friends visit gravesites. The nation recounts stories about the unselfish of contributions of these men and women who kept our borders safe so that we could sleep securely every night.

As a young man on a kibbutz, I recall reading a simple story on Memorial Day, "We Remember Jimmy." Written in Hebrew, it was the story of a young *kibbutznik* (member of a communal farming society) who was killed in our War of Independence. At first, I thought it was just a good story, something to pass my time. But as the story unfolded, Jimmy's friends talked about his life and his heart. I learned about his family, was touched his poetry, and read accounts of young people who called him their friend. For the first time in my life, I felt overwhelming grief over the fact that so many youngsters like Jimmy had been snatched away by the horrors of war and terrorism. I am sure some Arab families feel the same way about their losses.

In the face of terrorism, it is crucial to mourn as individuals, mourn as families, and mourn as a nation. America is doing this in the wake of September 11. There will always be grief and pain. Supportive friends, along with counseling and prayer, aid in the healing process. Our children will learn how to grieve as well. This can lead to normalcy and healing. As Dr. Betsy Weaver noted in her short article, *As Families, We Mourn*:

Everyone in America . . . will to a greater or lesser degree go through the trauma and grieving stages: denial, anger, bargaining, depression and acceptance. . . . talk with friends, people at work and family. Processing and reprocessing the trauma lessens it.[3]

Dr. Weaver writes to parents, offering advice about relating the events of September 11 to children. She recommends age-specific strategies to help youngsters cope with terror.

Teaching Our Children About Terrorism

How do we teach our children to not be devoured by fear and hatred? The world of the *shahid* is filled with such hatred. Will our children learn hate back? Will they become obsessed with revenge?

I will never forget the time when my six-year old son approached me after watching a television news report about a terrorist attack in Israel. "*Abba* [Hebrew, Daddy]," he said, "it is hard not to hate all Arabs." It was saddening to hear his remark. Yet, it was touching to know that a child so young could sense that there was a world of hatred out there into which one could be drawn, and that somehow, this world was to be resisted. My son sensed that we were not meant to live our lives hating others, including our Arab neighbors. That evening, my wife and I told our children that we will always try to respect every human being, regardless of their background. We let them know that God loves people of every ethnic group, including Arabs. However, we also explained that it is right to hate the actions of the terrorist in the news report, that it is right to pursue, capture, and bring him and his sponsoring organization to justice. I do not know how much of our talk my son understood but it was a conversation I will never forget. We walk a narrow line as we teach our children about terrorism. We want our children to know that terrorism is evil and should be fought. Yet, we also want to teach them that their lives should not be consumed by the kind of seething hatred for Arabs that the *shahid* harbors against Jews and Americans. Harboring a deep and burning hatred destroys a person, even if one's cause is just and true. May the Almighty give us the grace to not wallow in the mire of such a destructive hatred while successfully being able to continue the battle.

One of my sons accompanied me on a visit to the Majdanek death camp, in Poland, some years ago. After walking through the camp on blustery, cold day, we discussed what the Nazis' terror meant for us today. I closed our discussion with a recommendation, as an Israeli and a Jew. I said, "the Nazis were terrorists. In Israel, you know what we do with terrorism—we try to battle it with all of the resources we have. This is what we must always do. Resist it, fight and destroy the networks that support it."

I have deep respect for the parents of Israeli soldier and American emigrant, Nachshon Waxman, and their ability to fight evil while not becoming a part of it. In the late 1990s, Nachshon, a new soldier, was kidnapped, tortured, and murdered by radical Islamic terrorists. All of Israel was horrified. Thousands of Israelis gathered at the Western Wall in Jerusalem to pray. We mourned the death of one of our finest young men.

Shortly after their son's brutal murder, Nachshon's parents appeared on Israeli television. They spoke about their longing for peace between Israel and the Arab world and about their desire to see the end of all hatred. There did not seem to be any bitter animosity or desire for revenge in their hearts. I have the utmost respect for this mindset. I am not always able to achieve it each time Israel suffers another attack, but I try to seek ways of coping with our situation without becoming full of rage and wanting retribution. The way in which the Waxmans responded to their tragedy is a lesson for our children and for all of us.

In August 2001, Israeli surgeon, Ami Cohen passed away. The story of his philanthropy to poor Arabs in all regions of the Middle East is heartening. One of the most generous people I have ever met, his life demonstrated the fact that in spite of the suffering the Arab world has inflicted upon Israel, many Israelis still go to great lengths to help our Arab neighbors. Cohen provided free medical care and treatment to over seven hundred Arab children afflicted with cardiovascular diseases. He was the impetus for finding these children, funding their care, and bringing them to Israel so they could receive much needed medical attention. A close family friend for many years, his life was a wonderful example to my children!

During the Bosnian crisis, Israel was the first country in the world to welcome Bosnian Muslim refugees. *No Muslim country did this.* Why would a Jewish state invite Muslims to live among us? It is because we, a nation reborn after the Holocaust, understood their pain and suffering. In Israel, our children grow up learning about compassion and religious tolerance.

In Israel, we have very frank discussions about terrorism with our children. We talk about the subject in our classrooms and we talk about it in our homes. American schools and families should do likewise. As in the United States, a democratic spirit exists in Israel. This spirit prevails as we teach our children not to hate all Arabs or Muslims. I know this is the case, as I have been both a student and a teacher in secular and religious classrooms. Respect for human life, in spite of the threat of Arab terrorism, is always stressed. This is in stark contrast to the teaching of hatred toward Jews and Israelis that is becoming increasingly prevalent throughout the fundamentalist Muslim world. It is alarming to learn that even in countries like Egypt, a nation at peace with Israel, schoolchildren are being taught to hate the Jewish people and Israel.

Out of necessity, Israeli schoolchildren learn how to respond in case of a terrorist attack. They understand that this is part of life in Israel. These are sobering lessons indeed. Yet, the openness with which we discuss the situation is important to help our children deal with the reality of terrorism. It is my hope that American schools will become places to discuss this reality, educating students as to the best ways to combat terrorism. Education, open discussion, and visionary planning are effective ways to help children survive and live productively in our current world.

The security of our children's schools is an important issue. Israel has taken great measures to secure our classrooms. As a young soldier, I occasionally drew guard duty at schools along our frontiers. It was a privilege to help provide an atmosphere in which the children could learn without fear of harm. I hope the United States will find ways to provide school security systems that are effective and conducive to the learning process. Some have voiced concerns that implementing stronger security measures in American schools could lead to civil liberties violations. In Israel, there have been few, if any, violations of personal freedom due to the implementation of these systems. Israelis cherish personal freedoms *and* hold security near and dear. A good balance is in place. In his article, "Six Tough Tactics," French anti-terrorist expert Jean-Louis Bruguiere, offers valuable suggestions on this subject. It is heartening to know that the American Department of Justice has met with Judge Bruguiere for advice.[4]

The Torah and Faith

Ultimately, I found only one way to confront the fears that arise from living in a society that is daily subjected to terrorist attacks. How does one find the inner strength to persevere under these conditions? The answer is *faith*. Believing in a God who numbers all of our days, comforts me. As a teenager, my parents took me to lecture given by Elie Weisel. I remember his words clearly. He said that Holocaust survivors came out of their experiences in one of two ways: either they were thankful to God for being alive and wanted to cling to him, or they harbored a deep anger at God for allowing such suffering.

There is a time for each of us to die. No one knows ahead of time when that day will be. Until then, God keeps us alive. Having this assurance helped me make it through terrorist attacks as well as other potentially deadly situations in the military where I experienced God's protection. Bullets came within a fraction of an inch of hitting me and rockets exploded nearby, but I was not harmed. I treasure these experiences because they gave me the fortitude to believe that I can live my life one day at a time, trusting in the Holy One of Israel to protect my family and me.

No answer is adequate to explain why some of the warmest, most generous, or God-fearing people have become victims of terrorism—and why I lived through my experiences. I do not know why the automobile on the road beside me plunged over the cliff after hitting the oil spill, while I slid to a stop against the side of a hill and walked away virtually unscathed. There are no easy answers. I am not espousing a fatalistic attitude. It is not fine to do whatever one wants, thinking that we will all die anyway. We *should* watch out for ourselves and seek to protect our loved ones.

However, in order to have the inner strength to continue to live in Israel, to build my life here and believe in a future for my family, and that of our nation, I need to rely on God. Only he gives me the wherewithal to go on. He will sustain Israel, even through our human loss and collective grief. The Bible tell us:

He that watches over Israel does not nap nor sleep. (Ps. 121:6, author's translation)

I understand why Lisa Beamer, the wife of Todd Beamer, one of the those who resisted the hijackers on the fateful September 11 flight that crashed in Pennsylvania, continually referred to her husband's faith as the sustaining element in his actions. His faith strengthened him through the crisis, and was his only peace of mind prior to his heroic death.[5]

Many of my friends do not possess such sustaining faith. Some have great difficulty dealing with the reality of a living in a violent world. They often look for ways to escape, and become despondent.

This is the aim of the terrorists, namely, to make us frightened of living and of standing up for what is right. If we succumb to the fears, we are in danger of losing our moral and religious backbone. We cannot control what the terrorists do but we *can* control how we respond to them. We have the power to keep the terrorist organizations from winning their war against civilization.

It is important to be good listener when helping victims of terrorism. Some of the most healing and meaningful moments in my own life occurred when I listened to Holocaust survivors tell their stories. When others listen, survivors find meaning for their suffering through teaching the next generation the lessons of their agony. One particularly moving experience happened in Poland a few years ago. An elderly Holocaust survivor who told me that she was a relative of Israel's first president, Chaim Weizmann, related how she had suffered in the face of Nazism. As a teenager, she had become angry with God over the death of her friends and family. Since that time, she had been unable to pray.

After hearing about how some Israelis find strength to pray to the Almighty in the midst of our current crisis, she became very quiet. Tears slid down her cheeks. After a few moments of total silence, she started to pray her first prayer in nearly fifty years. I will always remember this occasion. The only prayer she could recall was the blessing recited when lighting Hanukkah (The Feast of Dedication) candles. At first, I wanted to tell her that she had spoken the wrong prayer, as it was summer and not winter when the Hanukkah festival takes place. But I realized that any prayer she prayed to God after a fifty-year absence *was* the right prayer. The content of the prayer was not nearly as important as the act of opening her heart to God.

My encounters with Holocaust victims have been mutually encouraging; each of us has known a brand of terrorism, although again, I do not equate my experiences with theirs. An elderly Holocaust survivor related a story that moved me deeply. In 1944, on Yom Kippur, which is a day of fasting and prayer, she was starving to death. She was given her daily ration of a few morsels of bread. On that day, she gave her ration to her friend. This woman told her friend that today was the day when she would triumph over the Nazis. Perhaps she would die from starvation or disease, but there was one thing she could do to resist Nazi power over her life. She could refuse to eat her food ration, honor her God, and fast on Yom Kippur. She did so and miraculously lived to tell about it.

Mourn with your nation and then take back your life! Deny the terrorists the power they seek. If you were deeply moved by the acts of September 11, resolve to live vigorously. Do not let that vicious act steal God's gift from you—his gift of life. Here is an encouraging bit of wisdom from a historic military leader in Israel:

He who dwells in the shelter of the Most High will rest in the shadow of the Almighty, I will say of the LORD, "He is my refuge and my fortress, my God, in whom I trust."
Surely he will save you from the fowler's snare and from the deadly pestilence.
He will cover you with his feathers, and under his wings you will find refuge; his faithfulness will be your shield and rampart.
You will not fear the terror of the night, nor the arrow that flies by day, nor the pestilence that stalks in the darkness, nor the plague that destroys at midday.
A thousand may fall at your side, ten thousand at your right hand, but it will not come near you.
You will only observe with your eyes and see the punishment of the wicked.
If you make the Most High your dwelling—even the LORD who is my refuge—then no harm will befall you, no disaster will come near your tent.
For he will command His angels concerning you, to guard you in all your ways; they will lift you up in their hands, so that you will not strike your foot against a stone.
You will tread upon the lion and the cobra; you will trample the great lion and the serpent.
"Because he loves me," says the LORD, "I will rescue him; I will protect him, for he acknowledges my name. He will call upon me, and I will answer him;
I will be with him in trouble. I will deliver him and honor him.
With long life will I satisfy him and show him my salvation." (Ps. 91, NIV)

What comforting and powerful words! They emphasize the fact that only God can give us the inner peace necessary to overcome fear. While on active duty, I always carried the words of Psalm 91 in my uniform pocket. The author of this Psalm, written some three thousand years ago, had also risked his life to defend Israel. He took comfort in knowing that only Israel's God could deliver and protect him.

Psalm 91 describes how I am able to live in a country that routinely suffers from terrorism. After I was attacked while driving (one of the incidents described in the beginning of this book), it was a challenge to take the same road home from work at night. But I was able to overcome my fears and do what I needed to do. It wasn't because I was armed or because of a beefed-up Israeli military presence in that area. It was because I knew that I could call upon a very real God to protect me—and he did!

Israelis live with the fear of terrorism. Any time my family walks outside our door, we risk our life. Attacks have taken place on city buses and on city streets, in schools and in shopping malls. Attacks against Jewish targets have also occurred in South America, Europe, and Africa.

While I was at a business convention in Cyprus years ago, a conference of the Islamic *Jihad* took place two hotels down the street. Then and there, they boldly declared their right to murder Israelis wherever they found them: in Israel, on vacations abroad, at business conferences in Cyprus—it did not matter. Although it was unnerving to hear that statement, it did not ruin my trip. I had a productive week of meetings—and inner peace because of my trust in the Almighty.

The knowledge of Israel's military superiority over our neighbors offers no long-term comfort. I am a proud soldier of the Israel Defense Forces, support a strong military, and help with police patrols. I do this because I believe in a strong defense system. However, my only peace comes from faith in a Supernatural Power who has operated across human history. This Power allowed Israel to experience a political rebirth after two thousand years. When terrorism rears its ugly head, we must recall our personal belief systems and challenge ourselves to continue to live by them.

Other lessons from Israel's history can be instructive for us as we struggle to come to terms with what is going on in the world. To some, it may seem primitive to look at the Bible for insight. However, the Torah tells us that our ancestors lived through similar experiences thousands of years ago. The conclusions they drew about their trials offer us hope today.

In *Parashat Vayera* (Gen. 18:1–22:24, one of the portions of the Torah read yearly in synagogues), we read about an encounter between Avraham and God.

> But Avraham remained standing before ADONAI. Avraham approached and said, "Will you actually sweep away the righteous with the wicked?" (Genesis 18:22b–23)

Avraham spoke with the Holy One of Israel in his attempt to plead on behalf of Sodom, Gomorrah, Admah, and Zevo'im, four towns God himself had marked for destruction. Lot, Avraham's nephew, lived in this area. Avraham's posture in speaking with God is remarkable. In Genesis 18:27, Avraham acknowledges the fact that he is a mere mortal, about to engage in serious conversation with Almighty God. The text tells us:

> Avraham answered and said, "O boy, I've dared to approach and speak to my God, even though I'm just dust and ashes [merely human]." (author's translation)

As Avraham spoke to the Creator about matters of death and life affecting thousands of people, he was keenly aware of his position and of the seriousness of the subject matter. In Verses 28–32, he questioned God's limits, continually recognizing his own fallibility:

> [Avraham] said, "Please don't get mad with me if I speak a little more. . . ." (verse 32, author's translation)

Nowhere in this text do we find the smallest hint of God being disturbed by Avraham's pleadings. Despite his fears, Avraham *draws near to God* (Gen. 18:23).

What an awesome encounter! Avraham, a mere man, advocated on behalf of his nephew before the Almighty God—and the Almighty God listened to him! We should follow our ancestor's example, approaching God with boldness when we need to speak about matters of life and death, such as dealing with terrorism. We have the freedom to pray for God's mercy for our countries. Those with faith in the God of the Bible have a responsibility to pray for their nations.

Although we do not know what God thought about his conversation with Avraham, we can be assured that Avraham's intercession mattered to him. The Torah records the fact that Lot was spared (Gen. 19:29). Perhaps this narrative is included in the Scriptures to let us know that God will listen to our cries of mercy. The Torah does not offer mathematical formulas by which to relate to the Holy One. However, we are encouraged to always pray. Examples from the lives of biblical figures provide moral lessons to help guide our lives.

While I was in the army, I began each morning with prayer in our base synagogue. Asking God for mercy was an integral part of my being able to help defend Israel against forces more numerous than ours. As I faced God daily, I was reminded of the fact that though I was a mere mortal, there was an Immortal Power I could call upon for protection and help, the Potentate my ancestors had counted on. He would listen.

I do not mean to minimize the plight of those who called upon God for help during the Holocaust, other periods in Jewish history, or even on September 11, and who were still abused or murdered. I am merely saying that in my short lifetime, the God of Israel has been a comforting presence.

The Role of the Clergy

One sector of the American population can have a very positive role in helping citizens to fight the feelings of fear and despair that are caused by terrorist groups. Jewish, Christian, and Muslim clergy can make a difference as they set examples and provide religious leadership.

It is fitting for clergy of all faiths to demonstrate moral courage and to unequivocally denounce international terrorist organizations, their sponsoring states, and financiers. By taking strong initiatives to oppose the harbingers of terror, the clergy will be setting a standard for those they lead. A cleric's inner resolve is a model for his people. American ministers, rabbis, and imams must stand for what is morally right. By doing so, they will be helping the United States in its war on terror. Religious leaders can act as "watchdogs," asking that the use of American funds be monitored in areas where militant Muslim terrorist organizations operate. American funds should not be used to support any overt or covert terrorist infrastructure. For example, the Palestinian Authority, which receives American government financing, broadcasts children's television shows that extol the practice of child martyrdom. "Sing of My Life as a Suicide Warrior" was a ditty sung by Palestinian children on a program resembling America's *Sesame Street*.[6] When this became public, clergy worldwide should have protested loudly *and* called for the cessation of all financial aid to the PA.

Additionally, American clergy can help allay the "fear factor." Terrorism's ability to disrupt and destroy life has caused panic in the United States. American clergy can encourage their congregants to pray, to speak honestly and openly about their fears, and to trust in God. They can organize seminars on the subject of terrorism, emphasizing the above recommendations as ways of dealing with America's current struggle. The real threat of more murders by terrorists unless an effective homeland defense system is installed is not mitigated by the above suggestions. However, the clergy's role in encouraging citizens to continue leading productive lives is crucial. As a professional group, the clergy can also voice the need for adequate security systems in schools and public institutions.

The American Muslim community could play a very prominent and important role in the war against terrorism. If they oppose Muslim and state-sponsored terrorism, now is the time to speak out *loudly*. Imams can and should lead the way. No gesture would be more appreciated by United States citizens. If democracy, peace, and tolerance are true ideals of the American Muslim community, then it is time for them to be brave, and to take a stand against the terror perpetrated by their co-religionists, as Professor Khan has admirably done. Organizations such as the Muslim Public Affairs Council could have a larger role in opposing the aims of the radical, fundamentalist Muslim movements because of their ability to address the general public.

People in all societies listen to their clergymen. Therefore, the efforts of American religious professionals are crucial in teaching society how to cope with the fear of terrorism. Religious professionals have a responsibility to lead the way in this area.

Practical Advice

We all ask the question, "What can I do to insure that my family does not become a victim of terror?" In the late 1980s, I visited family in the United States. Driving through town, I felt a strange sense of calm. The experience was different from what I was used to and I asked my wife, sitting next to me, if she felt the same way. "Yes," she said, "I'm not looking at every street corner to see if someone's about to hurl rocks at us!" My wife had pinpointed the reason I felt so strangely at ease. We did not have to be on high alert while driving. I was relaxed!

It is time for Americans to have a more sober attitude about domestic terror. I am not suggesting that everyone continually turn their heads 180 degrees while walking or driving to detect a terrorist. However, some good Israeli-style vigilance is in order. All United States citizens needs to understand that this is *their* fight, not just the fight of others.

For example, when traveling, any suspicious activity should be reported to a local authority as soon as possible. When I'm on an airplane, I always "size up" anything strange or out of the ordinary. Once, while waiting for a flight, I noticed a stuffed duffel bag on the floor, a few yards away from me. The bag didn't seem to have an owner. I found an airline security agent and reported the ownerless luggage. Security showed up immediately. The duffel bag belonged to someone in line, and they had simply forgotten to retrieve it. As an Israeli, I am trained to be alert to the possibility that such a bag might be full of explosive material about to be detonated.

On another occasion, while walking through an airport, I saw a clear security risk. I immediately reported it to the closest airport security official. I was pleasantly surprised when the agent thanked me for my vigilance and acknowledged my point. He said he would bring the matter up to his superiors. I hope he did. All citizens should lobby their elected officials for adequate security in all public places. Your elected officials will respond to your voices of concern.

In airports, at shopping malls, in government buildings, at major athletic events, at public parades, near schools or universities, on heavily trafficked bridges, in hospitals—*anywhere*—suspicious activities must be reported. These sites are targets because of the thousands of people that frequent such places. If one out of a thousand reported "suspicious incidents" leads to the prevention of a terrorist strike, it will have been worth the effort of responding to the other reports. I am *not* advocating paranoia. However, I *am* advocating vigilance.

All workplaces should have a contingency plan in case of a civil emergency, such as a terrorist incident. A method of personnel evacuation or other means of employee protection should be devised. The Academic Dean at the college I taught at in Israel worked out such a plan. It was clearly explained to all faculty, staff, and students during orientation at the beginning of the year. This plan turned out to be quite useful when a suicide bomber attacked a restaurant down the street from us. Thank God, it was not a school day! The fact that everyone knew the contingency plan helped to keep us from entering a state of panic. Speak with your superiors at work. Encourage them to develop a contingency plan if none exists.

I am glad that President Bush has beefed up security at America's borders. In Israel, adequate border security is a crucial element in our struggle against terrorism. Terrorist networks as well as individuals cell groups have entered the United States from abroad. It is always better to apprehend such groups *before* they enter a country. Without strong border security, a nation will always be vulnerable to enemy infiltration. Additionally, I hope that United States Customs officials will be better able to detect security threats at Americans airports. Improved methods of intelligence gathering and inter-agency cooperation can make a difference in this area.

Here are some practical pointers for fighting terrorism in your local community.

1) Report suspicious activities to local or national authorities.
2) Advocate for good security measures in public places, especially at schools, in hospitals, and at public events.
3) Develop an emergency contingency plan in your workplace in case of a terror attack, or other life-and-death emergency.
4) Be vigilant when in crowds at public places.

CONCLUSION

My remarks have focused on helping the average American gain an awareness of the major issues relevant to our war on terrorism. Israel and the United States are engaged in a battle against the *same* foes. Cooperation between our two nations in this war is crucial.

An understanding of the modern roots of Arab terrorism can be see by examining the political philosophy developed by the PLO in the 1960s. This philosophy has been intertwined with radical Muslim religious sentiments, resulting in the proliferation of today's terrorist organizations.

Terrorism does not have to obliterate civilization. It can and must be resisted and defeated through a long-term campaign against all terrorist organizations, their supporting nations, and their financial backers. As individuals, we can cope with the fact the terrorism exists in this world. We can still find a way to go on living productive and meaningful lives. Israel has done this for over seventy years. America can do this as well.

I pray that President Bush's strategies in combating terror will be effective. He has correctly analyzed the grave situation in which we find ourselves. The seeming resolve of the United States government and the resiliency of the American people impress me.

May that drive and determination work to your benefit. May the United States turn to God and trust in him at this time of national crisis. The founding fathers of the United States turned to God in times of great need. Both individuals and families need to look to their Creator. Calling on the Almighty God makes a difference. It has for me. May the words of the Jewish psalmist be real to us:

> God is our refuge and strength, an ever-present help in trouble.
> Therefore we will not fear, though the earth give way,
> and the mountains fall into the heart of the sea,
> though its waters roar and foam and the mountains quake with their surging.
> There is a river whose streams make glad the city of God,
> the holy place where the Most High dwells.
> God is within her, she will not fall;
> God will help her at break of day.

Nations are in uproar, kingdoms fall; he lifts his voice, the
earth melts.
The LORD Almighty is with us; the God of Jacob is our fortress. . . .
Be still, and know that I am God; I will be exalted among the
nations,
I will be exalted in the earth. (Ps. 46, NIV)

I try to encourage all of my family and friends who are enduring
terrorist threats to turn to God for hope, comfort, and peace. Only
by doing so will we gain the strength to live like human beings in the
midst of a cruel and violent world. Combined with unceasing political and military efforts to battle terrorism, this represents the best
course of action, in both Israel and the United States. In spite of all
of our hopes, and our two countries' military thrusts, the threat of
terror may not cease.

The Jewish prophet Habakkuk was acquainted with fear. Writing after the horrific events that befell the Kingdom of Judah at the
hands of the Babylonians, his words reveal the kind of hope avail-
able to those who trust in God.

Though the fig tree does not bud, and there are no grapes on
the vines,
Though the olive crop fails and the fields produce no food,
though there are no sheep in the pen and no cattle in the
stalls,
yet I will rejoice in the LORD, I will be joyful in God my Savior.
The sovereign LORD is my strength; he makes my feet like the
feet of a deer,
he enables me to go on the heights. (Hab. 3:17–19, NIV)

Our nations will actively continue to fight the war against terrorism. While they do so, we need to purposefully cultivate our relationship with God. Only then, will we be able to live fulfilled lives, respect
the dignity of others, walk in humility, and look forward to the future.
When evil seems triumphant and violent men prevail, these words,
written centuries ago, remind us where to turn for help:

Don't be afraid of sudden terror or destruction caused by the
wicked when it comes; for you can rely on ADONAI. (Prov.
3:25–26a)

APPENDIX A

The Israeli Declaration of Independence, May 14, 1948

The land of Israel was the birthplace of the Jewish people. Here their spiritual, religious and national identity was formed. Here they achieved independence and created a culture of national and universal significance. Here they wrote and gave the Bible to the world.

Exiled from Palestine, the Jewish people remained faithful to it in all the countries of their dispersion, never ceasing to pray and hope for their return and the restoration of their national freedom.

Impelled by this historic association, Jews strove throughout the centuries to go back to the land of their fathers and regain their statehood. In recent decades they returned in masses. They reclaimed the wilderness, revived their language, built cities and villages and established a vigorous and ever-growing community with its own economic and cultural life. They sought peace yet were ever prepared to defend themselves. They brought the blessing of progress to all inhabitants of the country.

In the year 1897, the First Zionist Congress, inspired by Theodore Herzl's vision of the Jewish State, proclaimed the right of the Jewish people to national revival in their own country.

This right was acknowledged by the Balfour Declaration of November 2, 1917, and re-affirmed by the Mandate of the League of Nations, which gave explicit international recognition to the historic connection of the Jewish people with Palestine and their right to re-constitute their National Home.

The Nazi holocaust, which engulfed millions of Jews in Europe, proved anew the urgency of the re-establishment of the Jewish state, which would solve the problem Jewish homelessness by opening the gates to all Jews and lifting the Jewish people to equality in the family of nations.

The survivors of the European catastrophe, as well as Jews from other lands, proclaiming their right to a life of dignity, freedom and labor, and undeterred by hazards, hardships and obstacles, have tried unceasingly to enter Palestine.

In the Second World War, the Jewish people in Palestine made a full contribution to the struggle of the freedom-loving nations against the Nazi evil. The sacrifices of the soldiers and the efforts of their workers gained them title to rank with the peoples who founded the United Nations.

On November 29, 1947, the General Assembly of the United Nations adopted a resolution for the establishment of an independent Jewish State in Palestine, and called upon the inhabitants of the country to take such steps as may be necessary on their part to put the plan into effect.

This recognition by the United Nations of the right of the Jewish people to establish their independent state may not be revoked. It is, moreover, the self-evident right of the Jewish people to be a nation, as all other nations, in its own sovereign state.

Accordingly, we, the members of the National Council, representing the Jewish people in Palestine and the Zionist movement of the world, met together in solemn assembly today, the day of the termination of the British mandate for Palestine, by virtue of the natural and historic right of the Jewish people and of the resolution of the General Assembly of the United Nations, HEREBY PROCLAIM THE ESTABLISHMENT OF THE JEWISH STATE IN PALESTINE, TO BE CALLED ISRAEL.

We hereby declare that as from the termination of the Mandate at midnight, this night of the 14th and 15th of May 1948, and until the setting up of the duly elected bodies of the State in accordance with the constitution to be drawn up by a Constituent Assembly not later than the first day of October 1948, the present National Council shall act as the provisional administration, and shall constitute the Provisional Government of the State of Israel.

The State of Israel will be open to the immigration of Jews from all countries of their dispersion; will promote the development of the country for the benefit of all its inhabitants; will be based on the precepts of liberty, justice and peace taught by the Hebrew prophets; will uphold the full social and political equality of all its citizens, without distinction of race, creed or sex; will guarantee full freedom of conscience, worship, education and culture; will safeguard the sanctity and inviolability of the shrines and Holy Places of all religions; and will dedicate itself to the principles of the Charter of the United Nations.

The State of Israel will be ready to cooperate with the organs and representatives of the United Nations in the implementation of the Resolution of the Assembly of November 29, 1947, and will take steps to bring about the economic union over the whole of Palestine.

We appeal to the United Nations to assist the Jewish people in the building of its State and to admit Israel into the family of nations.

In the midst of wanton aggression, we yet call upon the Arab inhabitants of the State of Israel to return to the ways of peace and play their part in the development of the State, with full and equal citizenship and due representation in its bodies and institutions—provisional or permanent.

We offer peace and unity to all the neighboring states and their peoples, and invite them to cooperate with the independent Jewish nation for the common good of all.

Our call goes out to the Jewish people all over the world to rally to our side in the task of immigration and development and to stand by us in the great struggle for the fulfillment of the dream of generations–the redemption of Israel.

With trust in Almighty God, we set our hand to this Declaration, at this session of the Provisional State Council, in the city of Tel Aviv, on this Sabbath eve, the fifth of Iyar, 5708, the fourteenth day of May, 1948.

APPENDIX B

The Palestinian National Charter, July 1–17, 1968
(Selected Articles)

Article 4: The Palestinian identity is a genuine, essential and inherent characteristic; it is transmitted from parents to children. The Zionist occupation (of Israel) and the dispersal of the Palestinian Arab people, through the disasters that befell them, do not make them lose their Palestinian identity . . . nor do they negate them.

Article 6: The Jews who had normally resided in Palestine until the beginning of the Zionist invasion will be considered Palestinians.

Article 10: Commando action constitutes the nucleus of the Palestinian popular liberation war. This requires its escalation, comprehensiveness and the mobilization of all the Palestinian popular and educational efforts and their organization and involvement in the armed Palestinian revolution. . . .

Article 19: The partition of Palestine in 1947 and the establishment of the state of Israel are entirely illegal, regardless of the passage of time, because they were contrary to the will of the Palestinian people . . . and inconsistent with the principles embodied in the Charter of the United Nations, particularly the right to self-determination.

Article 20: The Balfour Declaration, the Mandate for Palestine, and everything that has been based upon them, are deemed null and void. Claims of historical or religious ties of Jews with Palestine are incompatible with the facts of history . . . Judaism, being a religion, is not an independent nationality. Nor do Jews constitute a single nation with an identity of its own; they are citizens of the states to which they belong.

Article 21: The Arab Palestinian people, expressing themselves by the armed Palestinian revolution, reject all solutions which are substitutes for the total liberation of Palestine and reject all proposals aiming at the liquidation of the Palestinian problem, or its internationalization.

Article 22: Zionism is a political movement organically associated with international imperialism and antagonistic to all action for liberation . . . It is racist and fanatic in its nature, aggressive, expansionist and colonial in its aims, and fascist in its methods. Israel is the instrument of the Zionist movement, and geographical base for world imperialism. . . .

Article 27: The Palestinian Liberation Organization will cooperate with all Arab states . . . it shall not interfere in the internal affairs of any Arab state.

Article 30: Fighters and carriers of arms in the war of liberation are the nucleus of the popular army which will be the protective force for the gains of the Palestinian Arab people.

APPENDIX C

The Charter of Allah: Platform of Hamas, August 18, 1988 (Selected Articles)

Translated and annotated by Raphael Israeli, Harry Truman Research Institute, The Hebrew University, Jerusalem, Israel

In the name of Allah, the Merciful, the Compassionate

Introduction

Grace to Allah, whose help we seek, whose forgiveness we beseech, whose guidance we implore and on whom we rely. We pray and bid peace upon the Messenger of Allah, his family, his companions, his followers and those who spread his message and followed his tradition; they will last as long as there exist Heaven and Earth. O, people! In the midst of misadventure, from the depth of suffering, from the believing hearts and purified arms; aware of our duty and in response to the decree of Allah, we direct our call, we rally together and join each other. We educate in the path of Allah and we make our firm determination prevail so as to take its proper role in life, to overcome all difficulties and to cross all hurdles. Hence our permanent state of preparedness and our readiness to sacrifice our souls and dearest [possessions] in the path of Allah. Thus, our nucleus has formed which chartered its way in the tempestuous ocean of creeds and hopes, desires and wishes, dangers and difficulties, setbacks and challenges, both internal and external. When the thought matured, the seed grew and the plant took root in the land of reality, detached from temporary emotion and unwelcome haste, the Islamic Resistance Movement erupted in order to play its role in the path of its Lord. In so doing, it joined its hands with those of all Jihad fighters for the purpose of liberating Palestine. The souls of its Jihad fighters will encounter those of all Jihad fighters who have sacrificed their lives in the land of Palestine since it was conquered by the Companion of the Prophet, be Allah's prayer and peace upon him, and until this very day. This is the Charter of the Islamic Resistance (Hamas) which will reveal its face, unveil its identity, state its position, clarify its purpose, discuss its hopes, call for support to its cause and reinforcement, and for joining its ranks. For our struggle against the Jews is extremely wide-ranging and grave, so much so that it will need all the loyal efforts we can wield, to be followed by further steps and reinforced by successive battalions from the multifarious Arab and Islamic world, until the enemies are defeated and Allah's victory prevails. Thus we shall perceive them approaching in the horizon, and this will be known before long:

Allah has decreed: Lo! I very shall conquer, I and my messengers, lo! Allah is strong, almighty. Surat Al-Mujadilah, verse 21

Say: This is my way: I call on Allah with sure knowledge, I and whosoever follows me. Glory be to Allah! and I am not of the idolaters. Sura 12 (Yusufali), verse 17 (108 in Pickthall)

Structure and Essence

Article Eight

Allah is its goal, the Prophet its model, the Quran its Constitution, Jihad its path and death for the case of Allah its most sublime belief. Hamas finds itself at a period of time when Islam has waned away from the reality of life. For this reason, the checks and balances have been upset, concepts have become confused, and values have been transformed; evil has prevailed, oppression and obscurity have reigned; cowards have turned tigers, homelands have been usurped, people have been uprooted and are wandering all over the globe. The state of truth has disappeared and was replaced by the state of evil. Nothing has remained in its right place, for when Islam is removed from the scene, everything changes. These are the motives. As to the objectives: discarding the evil, crushing it and defeating it, so that truth may prevail, homelands revert [to their owners], calls for prayer be heard from their mosques, announcing the reinstitution of the Muslim state. Thus, people and things will revert to their true place:

. . . And if Allah had not repelled some men by others the earth would have been corrupted. But Allah is the Lord of kindness to [His] creatures. Sura 2 (The Cow), verse 251.

Peaceful Solutions [Peace] Initiatives and International Conferences

Article Thirteen

[Peace] initiatives, the so-called peaceful solutions, and the international conferences to resolve the Palestinian problem, are all contrary to the beliefs of the Islamic Resistance Movement. For renouncing any part of Palestine means renouncing part of the religion; the nationalism of the Islamic Resistance Movement is part of its faith, the movement educates its members to adhere to its principles and to raise the banner of Allah over their homeland as they fight their Jihad: "Allah is the all-powerful, but most people are not aware." From time to time a clamoring is voiced, to hold an International Conference in search for a solution to the problem. Some accept the idea, others reject it, for one reason or another, demanding the implementation of this or that conditions, as a prerequisite for agreeing to the Conference or for participating in it. But the Islamic Resistance Movement, which is aware of the [prospective] parties to this conference, and of their past and present positions towards the problems of the Muslims, does not believe that those conferences are capable of responding to demands, or of restoring rights or doing justice to the oppressed. Those conferences are no more than a means to appoint the non-believers as arbitrators in the lands of Islam. Since when did the Unbelievers do justice to the Believers?

And the Jews will not be pleased with thee, nor will the Christians, till thou follow their creed. Say: Lo! the guidance of Allah [himself] is the Guidance. And if you should follow their desires after the knowledge which has come unto thee, then you would have from Allah no protecting friend nor helper. Sura 2 (The Cow), verse 120.

There is no solution to the Palestinian problem except by Jihad. The initiatives, proposals and International Conferences are but a waste of time, an exercise in futility. The Palestinian people are too noble to have their future, their right and their destiny submitted to a vain game. As the Hadith has it:

The people of Syria are Allah's whip on this land; He takes revenge by their intermediary from whoever he wishes among his worshippers. The Hypocrites among them are forbidden from vanquishing the true believers, and they will die in anxiety and sorrow. (Told by Tabarani, traceable in ascending order of traditionaries to Muhammad, and by Ahmed whose chain of transmission is incomplete. But it is bound to be a true hadith, for both storytellers are reliable. Allah knows best.)

The Jihad for the Liberation of Palestine is an Individual Obligation

Article Fifteen

When our enemies usurp some Islamic lands, Jihad becomes a duty binding on all Muslims. In order to face the usurpation of Palestine by the Jews, we have no escape from raising the banner of Jihad. This would require the propagation of Islamic consciousness among the masses on all local, Arab and Islamic levels. We must spread the spirit of Jihad among the [Islamic] Umma, clash with the enemies and join the ranks of the Jihad fighters. The 'ulama as well as educators and teachers, publicity and media men as well as the masses of the educated, and especially the youth and the elders of the Islamic Movements, must participate in this raising of consciousness. There is no escape from introducing fundamental changes in educational curriculi in order to cleanse them from all vestiges of the ideological invasion which has been brought about by orientalists and missionaries. That invasion had begun overtaking this area following the defeat of the Crusader armies by Salah a-Din el Ayyubi. The Crusaders had understood that they had no way to vanquish the Muslims unless they prepared the grounds for that with an ideological invasion which would confuse the thinking of Muslims, revile their heritage, discredit their ideals to be followed by a military invasion. That was to be in preparation for the Imperialist invasion, as in fact [General] Allenby acknowledged it upon his entry to Jerusalem: "Now, the Crusades are over." General Gouraud stood on the tomb of Salah a-Din and declared: "We have returned, O Salah-a-Din!" Imperialism has been instrumental in boosting the ideological invasion and deepening its roots, and it is still pursuing this goal. All this had paved the way to the loss of Palestine. We must imprint on the minds of generations of Muslims that the Palestinian problem is a religious one, to be dealt with on this premise. It includes Islamic holy sites such as the Aqsa Mosque, which is inexorably linked to the Holy Mosque as long as the Heaven and earth will exist, to the journey of the Messenger of Allah, be Allah's peace and blessing upon him, to it, and to his ascension from it.

Dwelling one day in the Path of Allah is better than the entire world and everything that exists in it. The place of the whip of one among you in Paradise is better than the entire world and everything that exists in it. [God's] worshipper's going and coming in the Path of Allah is better than the entire world and everything that exists in it. . . . (Told by Bukhari, Muslim, Tirmidhi and Ibn Maja)

I swear by that who holds in His Hands the Soul of Muhammed! I indeed wish to go to war for the sake of Allah! I will assault and kill, assault and kill, assault and kill. (Told by Bukhari and Muslim)

The Palestine Liberation Organization

Article Twenty Seven

The PLO is among the closest to the Hamas, for its constitutes a father, a brother, a relative, a friend. Can a Muslim turn away from his father, his brother, his relative or his friend? Our homeland, our calamity, our destiny and our enemy are common to both of us. Under the influence of the circumstances which surrounded the founding of the PLO, and the ideological confusion which prevails in the Arab world as a result of the ideological invasion which has swept the Arab world since the rout of the Crusades, and which has been reinforced by Orientalism and the Christian Mission, the PLO has adopted the idea of a Secular State, and so we think of it. Secular thought is diametrically opposed to religious thought. Thought is the basis for positions, for modes of conduct and for resolutions. Therefore, in spite of our appreciation for the PLO and its possible transformation in the future, and despite the fact that we do not denigrate its role in the Arab-Israeli conflict, we cannot substitute it for the Islamic nature of Palestine by adopting secular thought. For the Islamic nature of Palestine is part of our religion, and anyone who neglects his religion is bound to lose.

And who forsakes the religion of Abraham, save him who befools himself? Surat Al-Baqara (The Cow), verse 130

When the PLO adopts Islam as the guideline for life, then we shall become its soldiers, the fuel of its fire that will burn the enemies. And until that happens, and we pray to Allah that it will happen soon, the position of the Hamas towards the PLO is that of a son towards his father, a brother towards his brother, and a relative towards his relative who suffers the other's pain when a thorn hits him, who supports the other in the confrontation with the enemies and who wishes him divine guidance and integrity of conduct. Your brother, your brother! Whoever has no brother, is like a fighter who runs to the battle without weapons. A cousin for man is like the best wing, and no falcon can take off without wings.

APPENDIX D

H.E. Mr. David Peleg:
Address to the United Nations, October 4, 1996 (Excerpted)

Mr. Chairman,

There is no single item on the agenda of this Committee that speaks so directly to the hearts of the people of Israel as the subject of the fight against terrorism. In the past year, seventy-two Israelis have been killed and hundreds more injured in a dozen terrorist attacks within Israel's borders.

For years, the international community's ability to effectively combat international terrorism has been hampered by two fundamental misconceptions. The first is that certain goals can justify or mitigate acts of terrorism. The second is that in the war against terrorism, neutrality is a viable option.

Today we bear witness to a growing awareness in the international community that the first of these misconceptions, that terrorism can in certain circumstances be justified, is a dangerous fallacy.

For decades, terrorism's apologists have tried to convince the world that certain goals are so hallowed that terrorist acts can be justified in their pursuit. But today, albeit belatedly, there is a growing consensus in the international community that no goal can legitimize murdering civilians and other innocents. Moreover, the international community is increasingly recognizing that those who attempt to harness cherished goals as justification for their heinous crimes are actually doing a grave injustice to the goals they pretend to serve.

. . . However, the second misconception—that in the war against terror, neutrality is a viable option for states—tragically remains far too prevalent. There are still many states which, if not in rhetoric then at least in practice, continue to behave as if they can remain neutral in the war against terror. This illusory neutrality can take on many forms–granting sanctuary to terrorists and their supporters, permitting the free flow of terrorist funds and the traffic of arms and material used in terrorist attacks, or turning a blind eye to the use of diplomatic missions for terrorist communications. Whatever the form, countries which fail to stand up and fight terror in all of its manifestations are by no means neutral. They are terror's accomplices.

... With the recognition that terrorism, whatever its motive, is criminal and unjustifiable, and that every state unwilling to be an accomplice to terrorism must actively oppose it, my delegation feels that international cooperation in the fight against terrorism must focus on three areas:

First: national measures to be taken by individual states. All states must recognize their responsibility to their own citizens and to those of other states as well. Individual states must enact effective anti-terrorist legislation that prevents terrorists from finding refuge and operating within that country.

... On the national level, states must address complex issues such as the abuse of charitable and social status for fundraising by terrorist organizations ... the abuse of refugee status in granting asylum to terrorists. When terrorist activity does occur, states must be vigilant and persistent in ensuring that those involved are brought to trial and sentenced with appropriate severity.

Second: measures to be taken on the regional and international level. On this level, we should learn from the terrorists themselves. Terrorist organizations have long recognized that they can only function effectively with a worldwide network of cooperation and informational exchange. The international community has been slow to realize that it must respond in kind: only on a concerted basis can we maximize the information and experience required to track and prevent document forgeries, to block the transfer of terrorist funds, and to eliminate the infrastructure that supports the continued terror and loss of innocent lives.

Finally: those measures to be taken by the international community with regard to individual states. This entails both taking firm measures against states that encourage or facilitate terrorist activity, and showing appreciation and support for states that actively fight terrorism. With regard to states that actively or passively support terrorism, the international community must make it clear: terrorism cannot exist in a vacuum. Those states that create the atmosphere in which terrorism can breathe will be made to pay the price. Concurrently, the international community must recognize that there are states for which the fight against terror requires extraordinary courage. These states must be shown that they do not stand al on the battlefields. They are fighting for all free and peace-loving states. We must strengthen their hand. . . . Terrorism is a global problem jointly faced by us all, regardless of race, nationality or religion. . . . Israel heeds the call of other responsible leaders to join in the fight against terrorism and its sponsors.

. . . The proponents of terrorism have many tools at their disposal. But there are two without which they cannot function: disunity amongst states and a lack of will in the international community. If we deprive the terrorists of these tools, if we are united in our will to fight terrorism, then together we will win this battle.

Thank you, Mr. Chairman.

APPENDIX E

Dr. David Friedman:
Private lecture, February 26, 2001 (Excerpted)

. . . Let me say from the outset that I am not unaware of the pain undergone by Palestinian Arabs. I spent three years of my life studying the Arabic language, the Qur'an, Arab history and culture while obtaining my Master of Arts degree in Arabic . . . In addition, I have visited Arab countries and spoken with many Arab students, colleagues and professors regarding their feelings about my country and my people. While studying at the Hebrew University, my Arab hallmate and I became friends, and had daily discussions regarding the politics of the Middle East. I do not speak tonight with an unconcerned heart toward Palestinian Arabs. I would affirm that Palestinians should have societal and political rights in Israel. However, I also affirm that the country of Israel is a Jewish entity, and this should not be compromised by dividing up our country and our capital, or by compromising the borders of our country. . . . Israel is our only country. It takes six hours to drive the country from north to south, and much of that time would be in the traffic jam that one encounters around Tel Aviv. It takes less than two hours to drive the country from east to west, if we include Judea and Samaria. Without those areas, which Israel is being pressured to give up, it would take half of an hour to drive the east-west axis in the center of the country. . . . Perhaps in other places of the world, this set up could be feasible. It is for San Marino, Andorra, and Monaco in Europe. But Israel is surrounded by hostility; our neighbors are not France, Spain and Italy, but Iraq, Syria and Libya. . . . That is our current situation. It is a tough neighborhood to live in. Our Jewish state of five million people is surrounded by over 200 million people in some twenty two Arab countries, many of whom are still debating whether or not we should have the right to exist. The Palestinians claim our capital city; the Syrians claim our northern border, with 33% of our daily water supply, as theirs. . . . Yassir Arafat's recent statement, saying that Israel is "judaizing Jerusalem" is absurd. Jerusalem is the capital city of the modern state of Israel. Jewish residents have inhabited the city for 3,000 years. That is when its judaization occurred. Only a short period of time under

Roman rule, and again after the Crusaders killed Jerusalem's Jewish community in 1099, was there any break in the history of Jewish residence in Jerusalem. In more modern history, by the year 1840 there was a Jewish majority in Jerusalem.

My experience with Jerusalem is an intimate one. I went to college there. I have lived and worked in the city; it is my home. My children graduated from its schools, and their best friends live there. My sons and I have had the privilege of representing the city in national and international athletic competition.

I have hurt with Jerusalem, too. When terrorists blew up two city buses in 1996, my cousin was aboard. With all Jerusalem, I wept. When suicide terrorists set off bombs on Ben Yehuda St. in 1997, a few meters from my office, I was in shock and I wept with the city and with all Israel. . . . The State of Israel and the Jewish people have a valid historical claim to Jerusalem, one that cannot be denied. . . . For some 2,000 years, devout Jewish communities in all lands of the Diaspora prayed daily in the *Amidah* [Hebrew, literally, "standing," set of eighteen prayers recited by observant Jews] and *birkat hamazon* [blessings recited after meals] prayers for their return to Jerusalem, and for the rebuilding of the city, as well as for the coming of the Messiah to this city. There are over seven hundred references to Jerusalem made in the Torah. Jerusalem has always been, and always will be, a central focus of the Jewish consciousness, both in Israel and in the Diaspora.

A charge you will sometimes hear is that Jerusalem needs division because Israel discriminates in allowing holy site visitations. It strikes me as rather droll that from 1948 to 1967, there were no voices calling for the Arab world to allow Jewish access to our holy sites in then Jordanian controlled eastern Jerusalem. And a good number of our holy sites were desecrated during that time period. Yet now that Jerusalem is under Israeli sovereignty, suddenly the Palestinian Authority and others are screaming for international control of Israel's holy sites. I cannot reach any other conclusion than that this is motivated by shameless anti-Semitism. When the Hashemite Kingdom of Jordan controlled east Jerusalem, Muslims, some Christians, and no Jews could visit the holy sites there. The Western Wall, Judaism's holiest site, was shut off to Jewish pilgrims. Under Israeli jurisdiction, there is no systematic discrimination in accessing the holy sites, such as Israelis were subjected to under Jordanian rule. Jews, Muslims and Christians frequent Jerusalem's holy sites. There can be no denying of this clear fact...The PA will not be satisfied with political control over part of a divided Jerusalem. I am saying this because I want you to see why I feel there is historical blindness and hypocrisy in the call to divide Jerusalem. Thus, I am quite concerned that our borders, including our capital city of Jerusalem, do not become untenable. . . .

I sympathize with a Palestinian desire to have a government to call their own, but am most disturbed at the quality of the organization that has been given the power to rule over them. . . . Yet we have to face the facts. The PA is not a democratic, freedom-loving entity. . . . The more area that the PA controls, the more it will spread its gangland, bullying style of leadership over such areas. If anyone has succeeded in portraying to you a PA that is democratic and akin to traditional American ideals, please do not be so naïve as to believe it. It sobers many of my people when we recall that the el-Husseini family, to which Mr. Arafat belongs, actively supported Adolph Hitler in World War II, and that Mr. Arafat supported the Soviet Union in the Cold War, and Saddam Hussein in the Persian Gulf War. Lest we forget, units of Mr. Arafat's army-in-waiting served with Saddam's forces in Iraqi-occupied Kuwait, making the PA's chairman complicit in multiple crimes. I cannot understand how the world conveniently turns a blind eye to this fact. . . . Mr. Arafat, despite his Nobel Prize, does not have a pro-democracy track record.

. . . Whatever shortcomings exists in Israel, I have observed that our Arab communities have the right to life, to work, to worship freely, exemption from military service and freedom of speech. Neither Saddam Hussein, the Syrian Alawite regime, nor Yassir Arafat can have that said of their administrations. . . . In the recent past, our ambassador to Finland, Ali Yahya, came from Israel's Arab community. . . . Nawaf Massalha served as Deputy Minister of Foreign Affairs, and hails from another of our Arab communities. . . . It's not a perfect [system]; we have lots of foibles. But at least we have been trying to provide our Arab citizens with legal (and civil) services, and have done so. We are trying. . . .

To understand how I view the present situation, let me briefly go into the past. Let me tell you a little bit about my people. The State of Israel was not created out of Jewish imperialist desires, as our enemies have often charged. It was not created for the end of oppressing anyone. All can read the beginning chapters to Dr. Theodore Herzl's book, *Der Judenstaat* [Yiddish, The Jewish State], and see that the modern state was created in order to save the Jewish people from constant historical attempts at our physical annihilation. The events of World War II proved that Herzl's basic assertions were true.

Other early Zionist writers whose works can be read, such as Moses Hess, Leon Pinsker, Yehudah Alkalai, and Zvi Hirsch, agree with Dr. Herzl's motivations—to save our people. There is a great appeal in their collective works to the humanitarian end of giving the Jewish people a chance to survive by returning to the Land of Israel. The early Zionist organizations, such as the *Hibbat Zion* [Hebrew, Lovers of Zion], *Hovevei Zion* [Admirers of Zion] and *bilu* [Hebrew acronym for "Come, let us go up"] envisioned settling in Israel in order to escape the anti-Semitism that plagued them. They also purposed to build a society based on their young and democratic ideals. . . . The one hoped-for peace with Arab neighbors was articulated by Zionist spokesmen, Ehad Ha-Am, Martin Buber and the State of Israel's first president, Chaim Weizmann. But it did not happen. . . . Please do not blame Israel for that fact.

It is easy to see that the buildup to today's problems could have been eased by the Arab world's acceptance of the 1947 United Nations Partition Plan. Such plan was rejected by the Arab nations of the world, not by the Jewish community in Israel. My point is that things could have been eased if the Arab world would have only tolerated our existence. . . .

The State of Israel was born in an hour of desperation, with a time clock ticking in our ears, with butchery and genocide being perpetrated upon my parents' and grandparents' generations.

Israel is not a perfect country. We can and must improve our relations with our Arab neighbors. But Israel is a place where the Jewish people have found a national refuge, and continue to do so. Some of the most moving moments in my life were when I listened to my Ethiopian Jewish students tell their stories of how they marched hundreds of miles on foot, fighting starvation, to get to a plane to find freedom and new life in Israel. I have listened to my elderly students tell their stories of how grateful they are for a homeland after enduring the hell of the Holocaust. Israel has been God's answer to Jewish refugees from all around the globe. 630,000 Jewish refugees came to Israel after being expelled from Arab nations during the late 1940s. Most arrived penniless. That is not a refugee story that is often told, but it is fact nonetheless.

My greatest concern expressed here this evening is that Yassir Arafat is not a trustworthy peace partner. . . . We had offered ninety percent of Judea and Samaria to him. The Jordan Valley and half of Jerusalem were in that deal, as well. We had armed the PA's forces with our own weapons to help make them effective in what we had hoped would be their Oslo-Accord defined roles. Israelis paid taxes that were sent to the Palestinians to help finance their state-to-be! By these actions, my people extended our hand to make peace. In fact, plans were being made to give much of the Golan Heights to Syria.

But how much can you give, when what you receive in turn is totally irresponsible behavior? How much more Palestinian violence will we be subjected to? How many more statements to the press will Mr. Arafat make which threaten my country? How much longer will Syria support, finance and house *Hizballah*, yet expect us to give them the Golan Heights? The recent behavior of the PA and Mr. Arafat is what has put the peace process into rampant disarray. There may be no hope left. The PA needs to totally reverse their way of dealing with my people in order to make peace. Given Mr. Arafat's record, I don't think the chances of that are good.

In spite of the current situation, I sincerely hope that my grand-children will be able to play with Palestinian children in peace. May God help us all to reach that day.

APPENDIX F

President George W. Bush:
Address to the Nation, September 11, 2001

Good evening. Today, our fellow citizens, our way of life, our very freedom came under attack in a series of deliberate and deadly terrorist acts. The victims were in airplanes, or in their offices; secretaries, businessmen and women, military and federal workers; moms and dads, friends and neighbors. Thousands of lives were suddenly ended by evil, despicable acts of terror.

The pictures of airplanes flying into buildings, fires burning, huge structures collapsing, have filled us with disbelief, terrible sadness, and a quiet, unyielding anger. These acts of mass murder were intended to frighten our nation into chaos and retreat. But they have failed; our country is strong.

A great people has been moved to defend a great nation. Terrorist attacks can shake the foundations of our biggest buildings, but they cannot touch the foundation of America. These acts shattered steel, but they cannot dent the steel of American resolve.

America was targeted for attack because we're the brightest beacon for freedom and opportunity in the world. And no one will keep that light from shining.

Today our nation saw evil, the very worst of human nature. And we responded with the best of America—with the daring of our rescue workers, with the caring for strangers and neighbors who came to give blood and help in any way they could.

Immediately following the first attack, I implemented our government's emergency response plans. Our military is powerful, and it's prepared. Our emergency teams are working in New York City and Washington, D.C. to help with local rescue efforts.

Our first priority is to get help to those who have been injured, and to take every precaution to protect our citizens at home and around the world from further attacks.

The functions of our government continue without interruption. Federal agencies in Washington, which had to be evacuated today, are reopening for essential personnel tonight, and will be open for business tomorrow. Our financial institutions remain strong, and the American economy will be open for business, as well.

The search is underway for those who are behind these evil acts. I've directed the full resources of our intelligence and law enforcement communities to find those responsible and to bring them to justice. We will make no distinction between the terrorists who committed these acts and those who harbor them.

I appreciate so very much the members of Congress who have joined me in strongly condemning these attacks. And on behalf of the American people, I thank the many world leaders who have called to offer their condolences and assistance.

America and our friends and allies join with all those who want peace and security in the world, and we stand together to win the war against terrorism. Tonight, I ask for your prayers for all those who grieve, for the children whose worlds have been shattered, for all whose sense of safety and security have been threatened. And I pray they will be comforted by a Power greater than any of us, spoken through the ages in Psalm 23: "Even though I walk through the valley of the shadow of death, I fear no evil. You are with me."

This is a day when all Americans from every walk of life unite in our resolve for justice and peace. America has stood down enemies before, and we will do so this time. None of us will ever forget this day. Yet, we go forward to defend freedom and all that is good and just in our world.

Thank you. Good night and God bless America.

APPENDIX G

Prime Minister Ariel Sharon:
Address to the Nation of Israel, March 31, 2002
(Translation from Hebrew)

(*This address took place after the terror attacks in the northern town of Haifa and the Jewish settlement of Efrat in the West Bank.*)

Citizens of Israel:

The state of Israel is in a war, a war against terrorism. This is a war that was imposed on us. It is not a war that we decided to embark upon. This is a war over our home.

The state of Israel, under my direction, made all the efforts to arrive at a cease-fire. All the time, since I was elected, in the midst of a wave of Palestinian terror, we placed before us the goal of doing everything to achieve calm and arrive at political accords.

We cooperated with the U.S. envoy, Anthony Zinni, and we received terrorism in return. We acted together with Vice President Dick Cheney, and we received terrorism in return. We decided to advance the prospects of a cease-fire and concede my demand for seven days of quiet, and we received terrorism in return. We withdrew military forces from the cities, and we received terrorism in return. Everything we received in return for our efforts was terrorism, terrorism and more terrorism.

We must fight against this terrorism, fight with no compromise, pull up these wild plants by the roots, smash their infrastructure, because there is no compromise with terrorism. It is impossible to compromise with one who is prepared—like the suicide bombers on the streets of Israel's cities and in the twin towers in the United States—to die only to kill innocent civilians, children, women and infants, to die in order to cause fear and horror.

This terrorism is activated, directed and initiated by one man: the chairman of the Palestinian Authority, Yasir Arafat. Arafat is at the head of a coalition of terrorism. He operates a strategy of terrorism. The chairman of the Palestinian Authority is an enemy of Israel. He is the enemy of the entire free world. Everyone who seeks freedom, everyone who was brought up on the values of freedom and democracy must know that Arafat is an obstacle to peace in the Mideast. Arafat is a danger to the whole region.

The Israeli government decided at its meeting on Thursday to begin a wide-ranging operation to root out the terrorist infrastructure in the Palestinian territories. We will clean out the terrorist infrastructure from the foundations, because in the end we know that the only way to reach a cease-fire, negotiations, an accord, an agreement and peace is if we succeed in wiping out the terrorism infrastructure.

The state of Israel seeks peace. Our hand is and always will be extended for peace with the Palestinian people and the people of the whole region. But no one should be deluded. Our extended hand does not mean that we will give in to terrorism or to terrorists.

Citizens of Israel: The state of Israel stands at a crossroads of its history. The situation is not easy, but we have known worse situations than this, and we overcame them all. This time, too, we will emerge victorious. This time, too, we will win, and when that happens, we will be able to live here together in peace.

ENDNOTES

Introduction

[1] Herb Keinon, "Sharon Declares Day of Mourning." Jerusalem Post. 12 October 2001. <http://www.pqasb.pqarchives.com/post> (10 November 2001).

[2] Robert Tracinski. "We Are All Israelis Now." 20 October 2001. <http://www.aynrand.org/medialink/columns/rt091801.shtml> (1 November 2001).

[3] Keinon. "Sharon Declares Day of Mourning."

Chapter One

[1] D. Dorris, E-mail to the author. 29 October 2001.

[2] Israel Defense Forces. "Statistics." 1996–2002. <http://www.idf.il/English/news/jump_2_eng300900.stm> (21 April 2002).

[3] George W. Bush. "Address to the Nation."

Chapter Three

[1] Muhsin Khan, translator. "Sahih Bukhari." <http://www.iiu.edu.my/deed/hadith/bukhari/001_sbt.html> (1 April 2001).

[2] S. Abu 'Ala Maududi. Chapter Introductions to the Quran." <http://www.unn.ac.uk/societies/Islamic/quran/intro/index.htm> (1 November 2001).

Chapter Four

[1] Anwar Ibn Najeeb. Private Lecture.

[2] Ibn Najeeb. Private Lecture.

[3] Selengut 104.

[4] Selengut 112–113.

[5] Netanyahu 129.

[6] M.Z. Shabazz. C-SPAN Television. 31 October 2001.

[7] Bryan Curtis. "Four Thousand Jews, One Lie." 5 October 2001. '<http://www.slate.msn.com/?id=116813> (20 October 2001).

8   Muqtedar Khan. "Memo to American Muslims." 19 October 2001.
     <http://ijtihad.org/memo.htm> (20 October 2001).
9   American-Israel Public Affairs Committee. "Near East Report." 22
     October 2001.
     <http://www.aipac.org/neareastreport.cfm> (12 November 2001).
10   Thomas Friedman. "Fighting bin Ladenism." 6 November 2001.
     <http://aipac.org/documents/friedman1106.html> (1 March 2002).
11   Selengut 102–18.
12   Middle Eastern Media and Research Institute. *Special Dispatch 295.*
     <http://www.memri.org/sd/SP29101.html> (19 May 2002).
13   Ahmad Abu Halabiya. "Kill All The Jews." 13 October 2000.
     <http://www.adl.org/israel/mosque_sermon.html
     (20 September 2001).
14   Abu Halabiya. "Kill All The Jews."
15   Itamar Marcus. "Studies on Palestinian Culture and Society." *Special
     Report Number 37.* 2 July 2001.
     <http://www.pmw.org.il/report-37.html> (1 March 2002).
16   Abu Halabiya. "Kill All The Jews."
17   Abu Halabiya. "Kill All The Jews."
18   Abu Halabiya. "Kill All The Jews."
19   Itamar Marcus. "Murder, Rape, Violence and War for Allah Against the
     Jews." *Special Report Number 30.* 24 September 2000.
     <http://pmw.org.il/report-30.html> (14 September 2001).
20   Marcus. "Murder, Rape, Violence and War for Allah Against the Jews."
21   Abu Halabiya. "Kill All The Jews."
22   Abu Halabiya. "Kill All The Jews."
23   Abu Halabiya. "Kill All The Jews."
24   Abu Halabiya. "Kill All The Jews."
25   Sheik Isma'il Al-Ghadwan, Palestinian Broadcasting Authority televi-
     sion sermon. 17 August 2001.
26   Itamar Marcus. "Call to Kill Jews and Conquer Israel in Palestinian TV
     Sermon." 8 August 2001.
     <http://www.pmw.org.il/sitem-080801.html> (10 November 2001).

Chapter Five

1 Israel Defense Forces. "Statistics." 1996–2002.
     <http://www.idf.il/English/news/jump_2_eng300900.stm> (21 April
     2002).

2   Israel Broadcasting Authority report. "mabat lehadashot." 30 October 2001.

3   Tracinski. "We Are All Israelis Now."

4   Avalon Project at the Yale Law School. "The Palestine National Charter: Resolutions of the Palestine National Council, July 1–17, 1968." 1996. <http://www.yale.edu/lawweb/Avalon/Mideast/plocov.htm> (2 October 2001).

5   M. Dorf. "Congress seeks to cut funds to Palestinian TV." 21 April 1998. <http://www.Likud.nl/extr40.html> (26 March 2002).

6   Avalon Project at the Yale Law School. "The Palestine National Charter: Resolutions of the Palestine National Council, July 1–17, 1968."

7   Avalon Project at the Yale Law School. "The Palestine National Charter: Resolutions of the Palestine National Council, July 1–17, 1968."

8   Information Regarding Israel's Security. *Quote Sheet Number 30*. 15 October 2001. <http://www.iris.org/il/quotes/quote30.htm> (9 February 2002).

9   Information Regarding Israel's Security. *Quote Sheet Number 30*.

10   Information Regarding Israel's Security. *Quote Sheet Number 30*.

11   Associated Press. "Text of Osama bin Laden's Statement." 24 September 2001. <http://www.usatoday.com/news/nation/2001/09/24/binladen-text.htm> (25 September 2001).

Chapter Six

1   George W. Bush. "Address to the Nation." World Congress Center, Atlanta, GA. 8 November 2001. <http://whitehouse.gov/news/releases/2001/11/20011108-13. html.> (9 November 2001).

2   George W. Bush. "Address to the Nation."

3   Tracinski. "We Are All Israelis Now."

4   Amos Harel. "Bin Laden long reach into Israel-PA tried to protect Bin Laden's agent." 14 September 2001. <http://www.freerepublic.com/focus/news530579/posts> (22 March 2002).

5   Thomas Friedman. "Fighting bin Ladenism." 6 November 2001. <http://www.aipac.org/documents/friedman1106.html> (1 March 2002).

6   Norman Podhoretz. "Israel Isn't the Issue." 12 November 2001. <http://www.Netanyahu.org/is.htm> (1 April 2002).

7   Tracinski. "We Are All Israelis Now."

8   Marcus. "Rape, Murder, Violence and War for Allah Against the Jews."

9   Information Regarding Israel's Security. *Quote Sheet Number 30.*

10   Information Regarding Israel's Security. *Quote Sheet Number 30.*

11   Middle Eastern Media and Research Institute, *Special Dispatch 291.*

12   Middle Eastern Media and Research Institute, *Special Dispatch 291.*

13   Dietrich Alexander and Jacques Schuster. "Israel is no pariah in
     Europe." *Ha'aretz Daily.* 6 November 2001.
     <http://haaretzdaily.com/hasen/pages/ShArt.jhtml?itemNo=91396
     &contrassID=2&subContrassID=1&sbSubContrassID=0
     &listSoc=y> (12 May 2002).

14   Leslie Katz. "Don't Blame Israel for Embassy hits, area scholar says."
     Northern California Jewish Bulletin. 28 August 1998.
     <http://jewishsf.com/bk980828/sfablame.htm> (1 April 2002).

15   *Irish Times.* "Military campaign primarily a religious war—bin Laden."
     3 November 2001.
     <http://www.ireland.com%2Fnewspaper%2Farchive%2Findex.htm>
     (19 November 2001).

16   Fiamma Nirenstein. "How Suicide Bombers are Made," 53.

17   Anthony Cordesman. "Responses to Terrorism Seminar."

18   Calahan 5.

19   Cordesman. "Responses to Terrorism Seminar."

20   George W. Bush. "Address to Congress by President George Bush on
     September 20, 2001."
     <http://www.september11news.com/PresidentBush.htm>
     (21 September 2001).

21   George W. Bush. "Address to Congress by President George Bush on
     September 20, 2001."

22   American-Israel Public Affairs Committee. "Near East Report." 22
     October 2001.
     <http://www.aipac.org/neareastreport.cfm> (12 November 2001).

23   Joseph Aaron. "Night of Infamy." *Chicago Jewish News Online: Archives.*
     28 September 2001.
     <http://www.chicagojewishnews.com/archives_articles.jsp?id=10517>
     (10 April 2002).

24   Dietrich Alexander and Jacques Schuster. "Israel is no pariah in
     Europe."

Chapter Seven

1   William Safire. "For a Muslim Legion." 1 May 2002.
     <http://www.insteadof.com/TerrorAttack/p.39.htm> (20 May 2002).

2   Safire. "For a Muslim Legion."

3   *Ma'ariv Daily.* Editorial Staff. "seker shel muslimim britim". (2 November 2001): 1.

4   Middle Eastern Media and Research Institute. *Special Dispatch 292.*

5   Middle Eastern Media and Research Institute. *Special Dispatch 292.*

6   Middle Eastern Media and Research Institute. *Special Dispatch 292.*

7   Royal Embassy of Saudi Arabia. "Two Nations. One Goal." Advertisement. *Boston Globe.* (10 December 2001): A9.

8   Middle Eastern Media and Research Institute. *Special Dispatch 349.*

9   Jerusalem Post Online. "Saudi Arabia Offers Complete Peace to Israel." 13 March 2002.
     <http://pqasb.pqarchiver.com/jpost> (14 March 2002).

10   Middle Eastern Media and Research Institute. *Special Dispatch 354.*

11   David Dolan. "Despising America." 23 March 2002.
     <http://www.ddolan.com> (1 April 2002).

12   Robert McFarlane. "Responses to Terrorism Seminar."

13   L. Paul Bremer. "Responses to Terrorism Seminar."

14   Middle Eastern Media and Research Institute. *Special Dispatch 292.*

15   Middle Eastern Media and Research Institute. *Special Dispatch 292.*

16   Middle Eastern Media and Research Institute. *Special Dispatch 292.*

17   Walter Laqueur. "The Conventional Wisdom is Wrong." 3 October 2001.
     <http://www.gamla.org.il/english/article/2001/oct/lq.htm>
     (5 October 2001).

18   Middle Eastern Media and Research Institute. *Special Dispatch 265.*

19   Middle Eastern Media and Research Institute. *Special Dispatch 281.*

20   American-Israel Public Affairs Committee. *Near East Report.* 22 October 2001.
     <http://www.aipac.org/neareastreport.cfm> (12 November 2001).

21   American-Israel Public Affairs Committee. *Near East Report.* 22 October 2001.

22   American-Israel Public Affairs Committee. *Near East Report.* 22 October 2001.

23   Middle Eastern Media and Research Institute. *Special Dispatch 275.*

[24] Middle Eastern Media and Research Institute. *Special Dispatch 275.*

[25] Riaz Khan. "Pakistanis Leave for Holy War." 27 October 2001. <http://www.oureffort.2001.com/RESEARCH/TALIBAN/pakholywar.htm> (1 June 2002).

[26] Associated Press. "Turkey to send special forces to Afghanistan to train northern alliance." 1 November 2001. <http://abcnews.go.com/wire/World/ap20011101_412.htm> (14 March 2002).

[27] Netanyahu 125.

Chapter Eight

[1] Elie Wiesel. "We Choose Honor." 28 October 2001. <http://www.poynter.org/dr_ink/wiesel.htm> (4 April 2002).

[2] Wiesel. "We Choose Honor."

[3] Betsy Weaver. "As Parents, We Mourn," 25–26.

[4] Jean-Louis Bruguiere. "Six Tough Tactics," 167–168.

[5] Beamer, Lisa, interview by Oprah Winfrey.

[6] Matthew Dorf. "Congress seeks to cut funds to Palestinian TV." 21 April 1998. <http://www.likud.nl/extr40.html> 26 March 2002).

GLOSSARY

ADONAI—literally, "my Lord," a word the Hebrew Bible uses to refer to God. The large and small capital letters represent the Tetragrammaton, the Hebrew name of God, consisting of the four letters, *Yud-Heh-Vav-Heh*, sometimes rendered in English as Jehovah or Yahweh, but usually as LORD.

Allah—the Arabic word for God

Al-Aksa—a mosque on the Temple Mount in Jerusalem; also, the name given the current *intifada* (the *Al-Aksa intifada*), and a terror cell of *Fatah* (the *Al-Aksa* Brigade)

Al-Andalus—Andalusian Spain, the site of Muslim governments under which Jewish civilization was able to flourish for a limited time

Al-Qa'eda—literally, "foundation," an extremist Muslim organization that uses violence against Western targets to attain political objectives

Avraham—the Hebrew name for the biblical figure, Abraham

Banu—literally, "sons of." This Arabic word refers to the Jewish clans of Nadir, Qurayza, and Qaynuqa, and the Arab clans of Aus, Khazraj and Quraysh.

B.C.E. and C.E.—Respectively, these terms stand for "Before the Common Era" (B.C.E., commonly B.C.) and "Common Era" (C.E., commonly A.D.).

DFLP—Democratic Front for the Liberation of Palestine. A Marxist-Leninist, Syrian-backed organization that has dwindled in size and influence in recent years. It had been active in attacking Israel's borders in the past. This group split off from the PFLP.

Dhimmi—literally, "subjugated people," a non-Muslim population group living in a Muslim country, subject to a special tax

Fatah—literally, "to conquer," the largest faction in the PLO. This group has been the leading PLO power for many years, and is responsible for spearheading the current *intifada* against Israel.

Fatwa—literally, an "edict" issued by an authoritative Muslim religious council. In the eyes of fundamentalist Muslims, it is a ruling on a specific subject, which all Muslims are bound to obey.

Fundamentalist—In this book, this term refers to very devout Muslims who apply the recitations of Muhammad to modern times. Thus, this wing of Islam has spawned radical Muslim organizations who believe in the violent overthrow of Israel and the United States.

Hadith—a story or a saying attributed to Muhammad or his earliest followers, not found in the Qur'an but nevertheless considered by Muslims as authentic source material

Hajj—the Muslim religious pilgrimage to Mecca, one of the five pillars of the faith

Hamas—an acronym for *harakat al-Muquwamah al-Islamiyya*, literally, "Islamic resistance movement," a Muslim organization with many Palestinian members who are actively engaged in the violent overthrow the State of Israel. They have been helped and protected off and on by the PA.

Hizballah—literally, "political party of Allah," comprised of fundamentalist Iranian and Lebanese Muslim terrorists who are financed by Iran and trained in Syria and Lebanon, with the goal of attacking Israel's northern borders and wreaking instability

Holocaust—the Nazi sponsored murder of six million Jewish people in Europe from the late 1930s to 1945

Imam—a Muslim religious teacher, leader, or elder

Intifada—literally, "uprising," the name for the two campaigns of violence against Israeli civilians and soldiers by Palestinian individuals and organizations. The first one took place in the late 1980s, the second, termed in Arabic the *Al-Aksa intifada* (named after

Jerusalem's *Al*-Aksa Mosque), started in the summer of 2000 and has continued into 2002.

Islam—the religion of people who believe Muhammad was the last prophet, and who live by the five pillars of faith: *shahada* (creedal recital), *salat* (prayer), *zakat* (charity), *sawm* (proscribed fasting), and *hajj* (pilgrimage to Mecca)

Islamic Jihad—an organization of terrorists who see their war against Israel and other Western targets as part of their *jihad* for establishing true Muslim religious goals

Jihad—a concept in Islam meaning "struggle" against an enemy; often has the connotation of a military campaign against a non-Muslim entity

Jizya—the tax paid by non-Muslim populations that reside in Muslim countries. It is a sign of the non-Muslim community's submission to the dominant Muslim government.

Mecca—the hometown of Muhammad, and the city to which the *hajj* pilgrimage is made by Muslims

Medina—the city where Muhammad first manifested political power, and from where great gains in the spread of Islam took place; located in modern day Saudi Arabia

Muslim—an adherent of Islam

PA—the Palestinian Authority, that is, the civil administration of Palestinians under the leadership of Yassir Arafat

PFLP—Popular Front for the Liberation of Palestine, a Marxist-Leninist organization, founded by George Habash, and later led by Ahmed Sadat. Sadat has tried to involve the PFLP in the current *intifada*.

PLO—the Palestine Liberation Organization, a union of various militant Arab groups whose goal is to violently destroy the State of Israel. Yassir Arafat has served as its chairman for many years.

Qur'an—the holy writ of Islam, consisting of over 100 recitations of Muhammad written down and arranged by chapters

Ramadan—the month in which Muslims fast during daylight hours, and then eat after nightfall.

Shahada—the confession of a Muslim, consisting of the affirmation of Muhammad's prophethood and the oneness of Allah; one of the five pillars of Islam

Shahid—a religious martyr; any Muslim who has died, either in battle or as the result of suicide while trying to kill an infidel

Sharia—Muslim religious law, based on the teachings of the Qur'an and developed throughout the history of Islam

Shi'ite—a minority wing of Islam, which believes that only the descendants of Ali are the legitimate caliphs; the predominant religion in Iran

Sunni—the orthodox sect of Islam to which most Muslims belong

Sura—a chapter of the Qur'an

Taliban—the fundamentalist Afghani political party that seized control of Afghanistan in the mid-1990s, and was overthrown by Allied troops in Operation Enduring Freedom, in 2001.

Tanzim—literally, "organization," the armed wing of *Fatah*, loyal to Yassir Arafat

Torah—Hebrew word for the Bible. This word can also refer to Pentateuch.

Ulama—a group of religious leaders, teachers, or elders; equivalent to the English word "clergy"

Waqf—lands once ruled by Muslims, and thus, according fundamentalist doctrine, they remain Muslim lands forever. The nation of Israel falls into this category. Thus, fundamentalist Muslims believe that the current State of Israel is invalid.

BIBLIOGRAPHY

Aaron, Joseph. "Night of Infamy." *Chicago Jewish News Online: Archives.* 28 September 2001.
<http.//www.chicagojewishnews.com/archives_articles.jsp?id=10517> (10 April 2002).

Abu-Ala' Madudi, S. "Chapter Introductions to the Quran."
<http://www.unn.ac.uk/societies/islamic/quran/intro/index.htm> (1 November 2001).

Abu Halabiya, Ahmad. "Kill All the Jews." 13 October 2000.
<http://www.adl.org/israel/mosque_sermon.html (20 September 2001).

Alexander, Deitrich and Schuster, Jacques. "Israel is no pariah in Europe." *Ha'aretz Daily.* 6 November 2001.
<http://haaretzdaily.com/hasen/pages/ShArt.jhtml?itemNo=91396&contrassID=2&subContrassID=1&sbSubContrassID=0&listSoc=y> (12 May 2002).

Al-Ghadwan, Ismail. Lecture. Palestinian Broadcasting Authority Television. 17 August 2001.
<http.//radicalacademy.com/genarrettessay24.htm> (10 March 2002).

American-Israel Public Affairs Committee. "Near East Report." 22 October 2001.
<http://www.aipac.org/neareastreport.cfm> (12 November 2001).

Anti-Defamation League. "Sharon's Words: 'Israel Stands at a Crossroads.'" 31 March 2002.
<http://www.adl.org/israel/Sharon_speech.asp> (17 April 2002).

Arafat, W.N. "New Light on the Story of Banu Qurayza and the Jews of Medina." *Journal of the Royal Asiatic Society of Great Britain and Ireland* (1976): 100–107.

Associated Press. "Text of Osama bin Laden's Statement." 24 September 2001.
<http://www.usatoday.com/news/nation/2001/09/24/binladen-text.htm> (25 September 2001).

————. "Turkey to send special forces to Afghanistan to train northern alliance." 1 November 2001.
<http://abcnews.go.com/wire/World/ap20011101_412.htm> (14 March 2002).

Avalon Project at the Yale Law School. "The Palestine National Charter: Resolutions of the Palestine National Council, July 1–17, 1968." 1996. <http://www.yale.edu/lawweb/Avalon/mideast/plocov.htm> (2 October 2001).

Beamer, Lisa, interview by Oprah Winfrey, *The Oprah Winfrey Show,* NBC Television, 27 September 2001.

Bodansky, Yossef. *Target America.* New York: SPI Books, 1993.

_____. *Terror,* New York: SPI Books, 1994.

Bremer, L. Paul. "Responses to Terrorism Seminar." Lecture. Nixon Center, Washington, D.C. C-SPAN Television. 19 September 2001.

Bruguiere, Jean-Louis, "Six Tough Tactics." *Reader's Digest* (March 2002): 167–168.

Bush, President George W. "Address to Congress by President George Bush on September 20, 2001." <http://www.september11news.com/PresidentBush.htm> (21 September 2001).

_____. "Address to the Nation." World Congress Center, Atlanta, GA. 8 November 2001. <http.//www.whitehouse.gov/news/releases/2001/11/20011108-13.html> (9 November 2001).

_____. "Speech to the Nation." U.S. Capitol , Washington, D.C. 11 September 2001. <http://www.september11news.com/PresidentBush.htm> (12 September 2001).

Burns, John. "Palestinian summer camp offers the Games of War." 3 August 2000. <http://www.nytimes.com/library/world/mideast/086300palestinian-camp.html> (15 September 2001).

Calahan, Alexander. "Countering Terrorism: The Israeli Response to the 1972 Munich Olympic Massacre and the Development of Independent Covert Action Teams." Master's thesis, US Marines Graduate Research Institute, 1995.

CNN Interactive. 13 December 2001. Cable News Network. <http://www.cnn.com/> (14 December 2001).

Cordesman, Anthony. "Responses to Terrorism Seminar." Lecture. Nixon Center, Washington D.C. C-SPAN Television. 19 September 2001.

Curtis, Bryan. "Four Thousand Jews, One Lie." 5 October 2001. <http://www.slate.msn.com/?id=116813> (20 October 2001).

Dawood, N.J., trans. *The Koran*. London: Penguin Books, 1999.

"Declaration of the Establishment of the State of Israel." 2000. <http://www.newyork.israel.org/conny/inbep.htm> (14 October 2001).

Dolan, David. "Despising America." David Dolan Homepage. 23 March 2002. <http://www.ddolan.com> (1 April 2002).

_____. *Israel, The Struggle to Survive*. London: Hodder and Stoughton, 1992.

_____. *Israel In Crisis, What Lies Ahead*. Colorado Springs, Colo.: House of David, 2001.

Dorf, M. "Congress seeks to cut funds to Palestinian TV." 21 April 1998. <http://www.likud.nl/extr40.html> (26 March 2002).

_____. "Palestinian Children Goaded into Violence."17 August 1998. <http://www.csf.Colorado.edu/forums/peace/aug98/0067.html> (26 March 2002).

Dorris, D. "Re: Terror attack in Jerusalem." E-mail to author. 14 November 2001.

Dudkevitch, Margot, Keinon, Herb, and O'Sullivan, Arieh. "Government Freezes Cease-fire. Ben- Eliezer: There Are Situations in Which a State Says Enough!" Jerusalem Post, 4 October 2001. <http://www.pqasb.pqarchiver.com/jpostindex.html ?ts=1020613485> (6 April 2001).

Farah, Caesar. *Islam*. Woodbury, NY: Barron Publishers, 1970.

Fernandez, Manny. "Reaching the Frontier of Islam." Lecture. Boston, Mass. 1 October 2001.

Flannery, Father Edward. *The Anguish of the Jews*. New York: Paulist Press, 1985.

Friedman, D. "The Relationship Between Muhammad and the Jewish Tribes at Mecca and Medina." Master's thesis, University of Minnesota, 1982.

_____. "Introduction to Islam." Unpublished essay. 2002.

_____. "History of the Israeli-Palestinian Crisis, 1973–1999." Unpublished essay, 2002.

_____. Private Lecture. Las Vegas, Nev., 26 February, 2001.

Friedman, Thomas. "Fighting bin Ladenism." 6 November 2001. <http://www.aipac.org/documents/friedman1106.html> (1 March 2002).

Halsall, Paul, "Arabs, Franks and the Battle of Tours, 732: Three Accounts." *Internet Medieval Sourcebook*. July 1998. <http://www.fordham.edu/halsall/source/732ltours.html> (20 November 2001).

Harel, Amos. "Bin Laden long reach into Israel-PA tried to protect Bin Laden's agent." 14 September 2001. <http://www.freerepublic.com/focus/news530579/posts> (10 May 2002).

Haykal, Muhammad. *The Life of Muhammad*. Kuala Lumpur, Malaysia: Islamic Book Trust, 1976.

Herman, Judith. *Trauma and Recovery*. New York: Basic Books, 1992.

Hitti, Philip. *History of the Arabs*. London: Macmillan Publishers, 1970.

Huband, Mark. *Warriors of the Prophet*. Boulder, Colo.: Westview Press, 1998.

Ibn Najeeb, Dr. Anwar. "Islam." Lecture. Glasgow, Scotland. 12 November 2001.

Irish Times. "Military campaign primarily a religious war–bin Laden." 3 November 2001. <http.//www.ireland.com%2Fnewspaper%2Farchive%2 Findex.htm> (19 November 2001).

Information Regarding Israel's Security (IRIS). "On Terrorism." *Quote Sheet Number 30*. 26 January 1995. <http://www.iris.org/il/quotes/quote30.htm> (9 February 2002).

Israel Broadcasting Authority. "*mabat lehadashot*." Nightly News Report. Jerusalem, Israel, 30 October 2001.

Israel Defense Forces. "Statistics." 1996–2002. <http://www.idf.il/English/news/jump_2_eng300900.stm> (21 April 2002).

Israeli, Raphael translator, "Hamas Charter." 1989. <http.//www.cdn-friends-icej.ca/isreport/hamas.html> (1 October 2001).

Jerusalem Post Online News Agencies. "Saudi Arabia Offers Complete Peace to Israel." 13 March 2002. <http://pqasb.pqarchiver.com/jpost/> (14 March 2002).

Katz, Leslie. "Don't Blame Israel for Embassy hits, area scholar says." *Northern California Jewish Bulletin.* 28 August 1988. <http://jewishsf.com/bk980828/sfablame.htm> (1 April 2002).

Keinon, Herb. "Sharon Declares Day of Morning" *Jerusalem Post.* 12 October 2001. <http://www.pqasb.pqarchiver.com/post> (10 November 2001).

Khan, M. Muhsin, translator. "*Hadith.*" <http://www.usc.edu/dept/MSA/fundamentals/ hadithsunnah/bukhari> (10 January 2001).

_____. "Sahih Bukhari." <http://www.iiu.edu.my/deed/hadith/bukhari/ 001_sbt.html> (1 April 2001).

Khan, Riaz. "Pakistanis Leave for Holy War." 27 October 2001. <http://www.oureffort.2001.com/RESEARCH/TALIBAN/ pakholywar.htm> (22 May 2002).

Khan, Muqtedar. "Memo to American Muslims." 19 October 2001. <http://ijtihad.org/memo.htm> (20 October 2001).

Laqueur, Walter. "The Conventional Wisdom is Wrong." 3 October 2001. <http://www.gamla.org.il/english/article/2001/oct/lq.htm> (10 January 2002).

Larkin, M. *The Six Days of Yad-Mordechai.* Tel Aviv, Israel: IDF Publishing House, 1965.

Lewis, Bernard. *The Arabs in History.* New York: Harper Publishers, 1966.

Ma'ariv Daily. Editorial Staff. "seker shel muslimim britim" [Survey of British Muslims]. 2 November 2001, National Edition. 1.

McFarlane, Robert. "Responses to Terrorism Seminar." Lecture. Nixon Center, Washington D.C. C-SPAN Television. 19 September 2001.

Marcus, Itamar. "Call to Kill Jews and Conquer Israel in Palestinian TV Sermon." 8 August 2001. <http://www.pmw.org.il/sitem-080801.html> (10 November 2001).

_____. "Studies on Palestinian Culture and Society." Special Report Number 37. 2 July 2001. <http://www.pmw.org.il/report-37.html> (1 March 2002).

_____. "Rape, Murder, Violence and War for Allah Against the Jews." Special Report Number 30. 24 September 2000. <http.//www.pmw.org.il/report-30.html> (14 September 2001).

Middle Eastern Media and Research Institute. *Special Dispatches 212, 291, 292, 295, 349 and 354.* 25 October 2001. <http://www.memri.org/sd/SP29101.html> (19 May 2002).

Mordecai, Victor. *Is Fanatic Islam a Global Threat?* Jerusalem, Israel: self-published, 1996.

MSNBC Interactive. 22 November 2001. National Broadcast Company. <http://www.msnbc.com/news> (22 November 2001).

Netanyahu, Binyamin. *A Durable Peace.* New York: Warner Books, 2000.

Nirenstein, Fiamma. "How Suicide Bombers are Made." *Commentary Journal* 112:2 (September 2001): 53–55.

Palestinian Media Watch. Special Report 30. 24 September 2000. <http://www.pmw.org.il/report-30.html> (1 October 2001).

Peleg, David. "Address to the UN Sixth Committee by H. E. Mr. David Peleg, Acting Permanent Representative of Israel to the United Nations." October 4, 1996. <http://www.undp.org/missions/israel/terror/htm> (20 September 2001).

Peters, Mark. "What Do We Tell Our Kids?" *Terrorism Survival Guide* 2 (December 2001): 82–87.

Pickthall, M.M. *Meaning of the Glorious Qur'an.* New York: Alfred Knopf, 1992.

Podhoretz, Norman. "Israel Isn't the Issue." 1 April 2002. <http://www.netanyahu.org/is.htm> (2 May 2002).

Price, Randall. *Unholy War.* Eugene, Oregon: Harvest House, 2001.

Roth, Katherine. "New York rejects 10 million donation from Saudi prince." 11 October 2001. <http.//www.nandotimes.com/special_reports/terrorism/rescue/story/129855p-1358420c.html> (10 April 2002).

Royal Embassy of Saudi Arabia. "Two Nations. One Goal." Advertisement. *Boston Globe.* (10 December 2001): A9.

Safire,William. "For A Muslim Legion." 1 May 2002. <http://www.insteadof.com/TerrorAttack/p.39.htm> (20 May 2002).

Selengut, Charles, ed., *Jewish-Muslim Encounters.* St. Paul, MN: Paragon House, 2001.

Shabazz, M. Z. Emergency Town Hall Meeting. Washington, D.C. C-SPAN Television. 31 October 2001.

Shakir, Mahomadali, trans., *The Qur'an*. Elmhurst, N.Y.: Tahrike Tarsile Qur'an, 1985.

Sharon, Ariel. *Warrior*. New York: Simon and Schuster, 2001.

Sher, Hanan and Schecter, Erik. "Israeli Ingenuity Takes on Global Terror." *Jerusalem Report* (December 17, 2001): 34–40.

Siddiqui, Abdul Hamid, translator. *The Complete Sahih Muslim*. <http://www.usc.edu/dept/MSA/fundamentals/hadithsunnah/muslim/> (27 March 2002).

Stern, David H., ed. and trans. *Complete Jewish Bible*. Clarksville, Md.:, Jewish New Testament Publications, 1998.

The Holy Bible, New International Version. Grand Rapids, Mich.: Zondervan Publishing House, 1984.

Tracinski, Robert. "We Are All Israelis Now." 20 October 2001. <http://www.aynrand.org/medialink/columns/rt091801.shtml> (1 November 2001).

Weaver, Betsy. "As Parents, We Mourn." *Boston Parents' Journal* (October 2001): 25–27.

Weisel, Elie. "We Choose Honor." 28 October 2001. <http://poynter.org/dr_ink/weisel.htm> (25 May 2002).

Weiner, Julie. "A Survivor Again," *Chicago Jewish News*. October 10, 2001. <http://www.CJN.com/archivesarticles.jsp?id=10970> (11 December 2002).

Yusuf Ali, Abdullah. *The Meaning of the Holy Qur'an*. Beltsville, Md: Amana Publications, 2001.

Zakaria, Fareed. "Why do they hate us?" *Hadassah Magazine* (December 2001): 9–13.